A **FALCON** GUIDE®

BASIC ESSENTIALS® SERIES

BASIC ✳ ESSENTIALS®
SIT-ON-TOP
KAYAKING

SECOND EDITION

DENNIS STUHAUG

I00061834

FALCON GUIDE®

GUILFORD, CONNECTICUT
HELENA, MONTANA

AN IMPRINT OF THE GLOBE PEQUOT PRESS

AFALCONGUIDE®

Text and page design by Casey Shain

All photos courtesy of and © Ocean Kayak except pages 18, 23, 24, 33, 44, 46, 48, 50, 57, 67 by Dennis Stuhaug

Library of Congress Cataloging-in-Publication Data

Stuhaug, Dennis O.
    Basic essentials. Sit-on-top kayaking / Dennis Stuhaug.–2nd ed.
        p. cm. – (A Falcon guide) (Basic essentials series)
    Includes index.
    ISBN-13: 978-0-7627-3833-5
    ISBN-10: 0-7627-3833-2
    1. Kayaking. I. Title: Sit-on-top kayaking. II. Title. III. Series.

GV783.S86 2005
797.122'4–dc22   2005046028

Manufactured in the United States of America
Second Edition/Second Printing

To buy books in quantity for corporate use
or incentives, call **(800) 962–0973, ext. 4551,**
or e-mail **premiums@GlobePequot.com.**

*The author and The Globe Pequot Press assume no liability
for accidents happening to, or injuries sustained by,
readers who engage in the activities described in this book.*

Contents

To Suzanne, who has led me into far waters, and to Finn Owen,
who follows in my wake. They'll do to run the river with.

Why Sit-on-Tops?

Why on earth would anyone want to sit on top of an object and paddle it? The basic reason is simple: Sit-on-top kayaks are fun. Fun in capital letters, fun with an emphasis on adventure, on recreation, on skill, and on exercise. You can drift through lily pads, you can sprint down a straight line with sweat pouring from your face, and you can skip from eddy to eddy on a whitewater river. Now, a sit-on-top is not superior to its conventional kayak cousin. When you launch one, you don't carry with you hundreds of years of "serious" tradition. These are boats that despite incredible performance seem to

A bunch of friends on a bunch of sit-on-tops just naturally leads to a bunch of fun!

bring out the kid in each of us. They provoke follow-the-leader games and water fights, inspire a few minutes on the water grabbed from the middle of the day, allow you to carry one atop your vehicle as just a normal part of your day. The first people who ever sat atop a floating log and poled it along realized that the core of it was not so much that they were "boating," but that they were having fun on a boat—in this case, the original sit-on-top.

So let's go have some fun.

A sit-on-top is the perfect craft for exploring new waters.

Find the Right Sit-on-Top

To quantify the broad spectrum of sit-on-tops is to look at the entire universe of kayaking and say, "Okay, that's it. Whatever kayaking is, sit-on-tops are—and they probably do it better!"

Well, that's an exaggeration. Sit-on-tops represent a way of building kayaks and, even more important, a way of thinking about kayaking and paddlesports. Instead of encasing the paddler within the hull of a kayak, the sit-on-top allows you to sit unencumbered and in comfort on the deck of the boat. The hull itself becomes an air chamber that offers (at least to conventional kayakers) unbelievable buoyancy and stability. The result is a craft of surprising performance that is just flat-out fun to paddle, whether you're into serious exercise, drifting around a pond, or challenging the rapids in a whitewater river.

Just as with the rest of kayaking, the spectrum of available sit-on-tops ranges from extreme whitewater on the one end to rocket-fast flatwater on the other. Whitewater craft pivot on a dime and hand you back change, with quick acceleration and little inertia. Flatwater sit-on-tops are designed to go straight and resist turning, with inertia that gives them a long glide between strokes; as a result, they can munch through small waves and wind without staggering to a halt. The vast majority of boats are in the middle, blending some of the characteristics from each end.

These middle-ground general-recreation boats will turn fairly easily and predictably, will pick up speed with a few paddle strokes, will go straight without an excessive number of correction strokes, and will have enough momentum that they won't wallow to a halt the second you stop paddling. They just can't do any one of these things as well as a specialized sit-on-top.

What's a general-recreation sit-on-top like? Well, there are both solo and tandem models, with a few that can be paddled either way and that in effect have a third seat in the middle. A solo sit-on-top will be 10 to 14 feet long with a 26-inch to 30-inch beam. It'll have some sort of keel structure. Most likely it will be molded of plastic, and the hull will weigh up to fifty pounds. Most will have at least one hatch so that you can stow stuff below decks, and many will have molded wells in the bow or stern for lashing your wettable possessions.

A tandem will be 12 to 16 feet long, have a 30-inch or so beam, and tip the scale at seventy-six pounds or so. Some, but not all, will have rudders—but rudders in a kayak are intended to keep the boat tracking in a straight line rather than to help it turn. They counteract the effects of wind and wave on your hull.

Most sit-on-tops are plastic—specifically linear polyethylene, a material that is fairly easy to patch but somewhat soft and deformable under heat or pressure. Cross-linked polyethylene is more rigid but harder to mend. Fiberglass is a craftsman's material and tends to cost three times as much as an equivalent plastic hull.

The sharp point at the front is the bow; it cuts the water for the sit-on-top to pass through. At the bow is a toggle handle, a short length of rigid tube secured to the hull by a fabric loop—use it to pick up your sit-

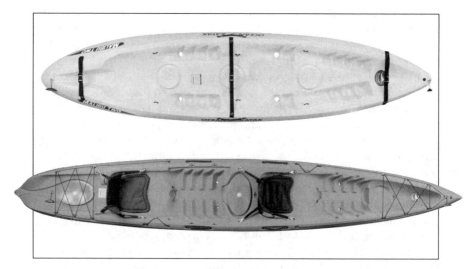

Different two-person sit-on-tops for different folks: The shorter, beamier kayak (top) turns more easily while playing in currents or waves; the longer, narrower kayak (bottom) glides more efficiently through the water in a straight line.

on-top or to hold on to it. Behind it may be a hatch, a well for gear, or a smooth deck. Footwells, next in line, look like notches kicked into the hull—but rather than your toes, these hold your heels. The seat is a divot shaped much like the mirror image of your own seat. A back brace— sometimes a seat, sometimes just a wide band—is a broad loop around the seat divot that keeps you sitting erect while it supports your lower back. Another cargo well or a hatch is behind the seat, tapering off to the back end of your sit-on-top. This is the stern, and it has another toggle handle. Most but not all sit-on-tops will come with a line stretching down both sides of the hull from the bow to the stern, a great thing to hang your goodies on, or lash them onto, when you're paddling. The rule of the sea is that if you don't tie it to your boat, it will wash overboard.

What are the advantages of a general-recreation hull? You can take one paddling for the day on a picnic or load up the hull for a week's cruise. Your speed will be adequate, you'll rise to most waves, and the boat will be relatively easy and fast to paddle. It will paddle easy—make that Class II or III—rivers, and it's a blast in moderate surf. In other words, it's a boat for all tasks.

Whitewater sit-on-tops are shorter, averaging 8 or 9 feet with a beam of 28 to 30 inches and a weight down in the mid-thirties. They have smooth bottoms, allowing them to spin and slide sideways. They may have just a hole and cork to drain out water or perhaps a small hatch through which you can cram air bags. You'll be able to kick one up to its maximum speed in one or two paddle strokes, and to crank in an extreme turn by leaning it up on edge and driving ahead. That's the whole idea of whitewater craft—to be able to accelerate from eddy to eddy, from tongue

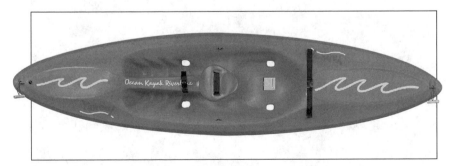

Whitewater sit-on-tops are short, making them easy to turn and spin. The rounded bows and sterns skid over the water rather than digging in and catching. Thigh straps or a center pedestal help you hold yourself in the boat.

to tongue, with precise handing. A rudder would only slow down your reactions to the current. The dream is to find a hull that is transparent, that becomes an extension of your body in the river.

At the other end of the sit-on-top spectrum are the surf skis, elongated javelins that rocket through flatwater or long ocean rollers. Singles and tandems will stretch out 19 to 20 feet, with maximum beam at the deck of 17 to 18 inches and waterline beams of just 13 inches. They might be made of fiberglass or a more exotic fabric, such as Kevlar, and will tip the scales at thirty pounds or less. The price for a bare hull will approach $2,000. Most will have foot-controlled rudders. One paddle stroke, and a surf ski will glide forever in a straight line; two paddle strokes, and you'll believe it's wicked fast. Endurance athletes can keep them moving at 10 knots for hours at a time—and they do just that when racing across ocean channels between the Hawaiian Islands.

Why the emphasis on going straight? Because every correction stroke to bring you back on course takes energy. Use that energy in forward propulsion, in going straight, and you'll cover more distance faster while expending less energy.

You'll rarely see a significant hatch on a surf ski, although some may have a small one for stowing goodies and pumping out the odd droplets and dribbles of water that sneak inside. I've found that a dry bag inside a mesh bag lashed to the rear deck works just as well, with a lot fewer complications and potentials for mishaps.

If speed is your need, climb aboard a surf ski and enjoy the fastest ride behind a paddle. Surf skis are the ultimate fitness and racing machines.

The first time you wiggle aboard a surf ski, you'll be convinced that it's too unstable to paddle. First of all, remember that it'll smooth out as you gain speed. Your paddle strokes will brace it. Second, when at rest, just take your feet out of the footwells and drop a foot spraddled on each side. That works just like pontoons—as well as like drag brakes—to stop any forward motion. A small subclass of surf ski is the one-person outrigger canoe, which looks just like a surf ski but has a stabilizing outrigger suspended out over one side. If you like high-aerobic exercise, these are a blast, and there are enough of them to make up competitive fleets in many locations.

A wave ski looks like a whitewater boat that has somehow been morphed into a flattened pumpkin seed. These crafts are short—7 to 8 feet, with a 24- to 26-inch beam and with a turned-up bow like a jester's slipper. There is a divot for your rump and a pair of loops under which you tuck your feet. The idea is to paddle a transparent platform out into the nearshore surf. That's right, you paddle out into breaking surf—on purpose—and execute a series of turns, spins, and other moves to gather points from judges on the shore. It's a worldwide, highly competitive, and highly organized sport. Most wave skis are fiberglass or a fiberglass composite—and, like any other highly specialized competitive craft, they have little room for personal gear.

Wave skis are designed with one thing in mind—playing in breaking surf and waves. Hone your skills on the smaller waves, though, before you challenge the cliff-hanging breakers.

Tricking Out
Your Sit-on-Top

3

Y our sit-on-top starts out as one of the most elegant and basic
boats that has ever taken to the water. At the same time, you
can easily and inexpensively customize it to meet your specific
paddling needs and desires.

For general paddling right off the beach, all you really need is a paddle,
a PFD (a personal flotation device, which is the official name for a life
jacket), and a sound-emitting device (Coast Guard and boating-law jargon
for a whistle, required by law). That will do you for your first voyage, and

The bare necessities—your PFD (personal flotation device) with an attached whistle, a bilge
pump, a sponge, and a towline/rescue rope. Every boat should carry these items.

If you want to carry anything with you—from a sandwich to a sweater—pack it in a roll-top dry bag and secure the bag to your sit-on-top.

for a lot of people it will suffice for their entire paddling careers. Consider, though, adding a handful of extras that will materially increase your creature comforts. A backrest will not only feel better after a while on the water, but also help you stay in the most efficient, erect paddling position. If you're paddling in placid waters and your sit-on-top has drain holes, think about stoppers to block the drains and give you a drier ride. If you're playing in waves or spray or you're really bouncing around as you exert yourself, open the plugs to keep your cockpit water-free. A paddle leash allows you to put your paddle down without it drifting away. Flotation bags—big air bags you inflate inside your sit-on-top—offer a tad of recovery insurance in case you accidentally lose a hatch cover, or even hole your hull.

If you're bound for more than a few hundred meters offshore, be it in fresh or salt water, you should carry a pump and a sponge. Condensation will form on the inner hull walls, a dribble will work in under the tightest of hatch covers, and there is always the possibility of popping open a hatch cover or even gashing a hull (I've had the cork work out of a drain hole.) Being prepared for a mishap is the best way to keep an irritation from turning into disaster.

You'll want protection from the weather and water, and that means technical clothing such as a wet suit or a dry or semidry suit—topped off with a hat or cap. You'll need a fairly large-scale chart of the area you're paddling, along with a waterproof chart holder and a compass. Binoculars will come in handy, too. Get a pair with the widest possible view and the brightest image—at least 6x30. (The first number represents magnification; the second is the objective lens size in millimeters. All other things being equal, the larger the objective lens, the more light it will capture

Sit-on-Top Kayaking

and the brighter the image will be. Wide-angle binoculars let you see a wider field of view at the same magnification.)

Carry dry bags to keep a change of clothes and food dry belowdeck; a smaller bag lashed within easy reach on deck can hold the snacks and water you'll want as you paddle. Last, and perhaps most important, you absolutely need a spare paddle. Some paddlers, attempting to save space, bring one spare paddle for every two sit-on-tops—that assumes you'll be next to a spare when you break your paddle. Some paddlers like paddle clips (clamps that hold a paddle); others prefer to lash their spare paddle in an easily reachable position. It's easier to find a place for a take-apart paddle than for a full-length, one-piece shaft.

Backrests (above) provide major comfort if you spend any amount of time on the water. Can't stow all your gear belowdecks? Place items that can get wet in a mesh bag and lash it securely to the rear deck.

Plan on Taking Pictures?

Any sit-on-top is a potential photographic platform—depending on the paddler's skill. Generally speaking, you're going to get better pictures from sit-on-tops in the middle of the design spectrum, because those will allow you to pay more attention to the camera than to handling the boat. Doubles will be more stable and less jerky than singles.

In every case you should either select a water-immersible camera (waterproof, if you will) or protect your camera or video gear inside waterproof housing. Spray, slosh, rain, an upset—somewhere along the line your camera will get wet, and a few minutes of protection more than equals the distress you'll feel when the repair tech says it can't be fixed. I find that a floatable point-and-shoot film camera delivers adequate photos. Mine has a simple exposure mode and four focusing zones, and while I might miss fine-tuning my images, I don't miss drying out camera innards. The digital revolution is paddling friendly. Check out dive shops and paddling stores for moderately priced ($200 or so) wet-proof digital cameras.

A Perfect Platform for Fishing

For me, half the revelation came at a misty dawn on Washington's wet coast with the quiet slosh of the Pacific and a breeze so slight that it barely rippled the water inside the jetty. The night before, a paddling friend had invited me fishing, and I assumed that at best we'd be jammed cheek-by-jowl on a party boat, or at worst sopped by the spume as we attempted to cast across the surf. Instead, as the dark drained from the sky, we met at the beach next to two sleek touring kayaks. Within minutes we were through the mouth of the jetties and heading north a few hundred yards offshore. In less than half an hour, we were tied off to kelp fronds with our lures in the water.

Paradise? Well, close enough. I was warm and dry instead of standing waist-deep in cold surf, I could fish at my own schedule rather than be packed along as part of the crowd assigned to spots at the rail, and best of all I could paddle rather than be relegated to passenger. The downside was that my tackle box, snacks, and all the bits and pieces that I leaned upon were well out of reach under the deck. It wasn't until I brought a red rockfish to the surface that I realized the rest of the problem—anything I caught was going to be dropped onto my lap.

But those were such little concerns. Bobbing gently in the slow swells, I realized that a universe of fishing grounds had opened before me. Coast to coast, lakes, ponds, and salt water, I could launch anywhere and anytime and within minutes be on the fishing grounds.

The second half of the revelation hit years later, the first time I saw people launching sit-on-top kayaks off the beach. They were beamy and stable; they had all that room for fishing gear—and, even more important, a place to drop a fish into rather than in my lap. I was hooked, so to speak. A half day in that first sit-on-top and I knew that I'd found my ultimate fishing machine.

I was in a bare boat, though. Let's turn that bare hull into a primo fishing boat.

Step one has to be paddle clips. These are springy C-shaped holders mounted on the hull that grip your paddle shaft and allow you to "park" your paddle while you're at rest. Use 'em when you're tied up to a kelp frond, and you won't see your paddle slip overboard and drift away. Equally important, the clips can hold your rod when you're paddling out to the fishing grounds.

One of the neatest gadgets is a D-ring or jam cleat mounted on the outboard side of the gunwale right about the midpoint of your boat. Since you can reach it by leaning just a bit forward, it's a great place to snub down a mooring line. If you're not tied off a kelp frond or the like and you want to keep from being blown all over the place, fly a small sea anchor or drogue—this looks like a handkerchief-size parachute—from that center point. Your sit-on-top will swing sideways to the wind and remain stationary in the water. If the water is moving—if you're in a current—you'll be dragged right along like any other piece of flotsam.

The stability and open deck design of sit-on-top kayaks make them the perfect craft for getting to your favorite fishing grounds—whether fresh water or salt.

BASIC ESSENTIALS

The Fishing Basics

You will need dry bags for your fishing gear and clips that serve double duty as rod holders (when you're paddling to the fishing grounds) and paddle holders (when you're fishing). A rod holder, to support your rigged rod when you're fishing, is essential and gives you the option of trolling as you move from place to place. A mooring line will allow you to tie up to kelp or other structure. You should have a bowline on your sit-on-top to secure your boat when you've landed on a beach, but in a lot of cases you can't reach that bowline from the cockpit while you're on the water. A lightweight, folding anchor and rode will hold you right over the fish. You'll most likely need a rode (or anchor line) at least three times the depth of the water you'll be anchoring in. For safety, a ¼-inch-diameter anchor rode is the minimum. For comfort (physical as well as peace of mind), a larger-diameter line—⅜ to ½ inch—is preferable.

Since you're not always going to fish off the same side of your sit-on-top, go all out and put one D-ring or cleat on each side.

My present boat has bow-to-stern lines running through fittings along each gunwale. If it didn't, I'd install them. You'd better believe that if you leave anything loose on your boat, a sneaky wave, a wake, or your own quick movement as you look from one side to the other will jostle that vital and expensive object over the side and into the depths. I like to paddle with a waterproof camera, and I've learned to tether it to my sit-on-top with a long lanyard with snap hooks at each end. I've also rigged a square of elastic cord, with additional cord crisscrossing the center, from small clips just ahead of my feet. It's a convenient spot to keep a chart protected in a clear plastic map case, one that I can make notes upon with a grease pencil.

A chart gives you a sketch of the area you're paddling; a compass allows you to take cross-bearings to both pinpoint your position and hold the direction you want to paddle. I've tried bubble-top kayak compasses, orienteering compasses (that familiar needle floating within a rotatable disk mounted on a rectangular plastic base), and bearing or sighting compasses. The domed kayak compass, mounted ahead of my chart, is easiest to use when you are trying to hold a course under poor visibility. The orienteering compass can be used to hold a course and take a bearing, but it requires more concentration. The sighting compass lets you accurately and quickly determine relative bearings to pinpoint your location, but it's miserable to paddle with. A global positioning system (GPS) receiver can pinpoint your location, the distance and heading to your destination, and the exact path back home. Get a water-resistant one and keep it in a clear dry bag.

Some paddlers like to festoon their boats with hook-and-eye fabric patches, with matching patches on their tackle boxes, gear bags, and bait boxes. It seems to work for them, but I like the security of knowing I've lashed every bit of gear securely in place with stout cord. That's why I've added a few D-rings around the boat, at convenient places.

My first sit-on-top had a solid hull—save for a drain plug at the end of the rear deck. It took a little more planning, but it was a perfectly adequate fishing boat. My current boat has a large waterproof hatch forward and a small, circular hatch amidships right in front of my footwells. Instead of an aft deck, it has a recessed and self-draining cargo well just the right size for a medium cooler and a pair of straps for lashing the container in place. Hatches are definitely the way to go, with a couple of warnings. First, no hatch and no sit-on-top are waterproof. Between condensation and seepage, you'll often get a little water inside. If you want to carry something that absolutely, positively has to stay dry, put it in a dry bag.

Because I'm a belt-and-suspenders sort of person, I have flotation bags inside my sit-on-top. I don't plan on losing a hatch or gashing the hull, but with flotation bags my sit-on-top will float even if completely swamped. If you look around, you can find flotation bags that open to house and protect some of your gear and then can be sealed and filled with air.

If you put anything down one of your hatches, it will slide to the most inaccessible corner inside your boat just before you need it. The solution? Tie a cord to whatever you're stowing below, fastening the other end of it near the inside of the hatch. When you want it, just reel in the cord. It still can get jammed, but you have a better chance of recovering it while on the water.

For serious fishing you're going to want one rod holder, and probably two—one mounted on each side of and just behind your seat. That'll keep your rod out of the way yet still within easy reach while you paddle short distances, and you'll be able to fish from either side. Rig another D-ring adjacent to one of the holders, and snap-hook the lanyard from your landing net to that. I use a short cord to leash my rod to a D-ring and avoid losing the rod to Davy Jones.

Now, if you've moored up to a drogue or to kelp, you'll soon find that even small wave action will have you jerking about as your line yanks tight and dangles loose. Consider tying two small loops into your mooring line, about 3 to 4 feet apart, and then securing a 2½- to 3-foot hank of stretchy elastic between those loops. The elastic will work as a shock absorber and mellow out the surges on your line.

Electronics can help put you on primo fishing grounds, but they also add a level of complexity that lifts you right out of the "simple" category. A good fish/depth finder will allow you to pinpoint promising underwater structure and can easily be mounted ahead of your footwells. If you have it near your compass, however, you'll find that your compass has lost its love of north. There are handheld depth finders the size and shape of a flashlight that will give you readouts of water depth and also offer a glimpse of the seafloor without requiring a permanent mount.

GPS receivers can guide you to any place you mark on a chart—and guide you back to any point you've selected. They're a super tool for finding your way home if you're caught in a sudden fog. I know, we're all supposed to pay attention to the weather every moment we're on the water, but the GPS falls right into the belt-and-suspenders rule of safety. You should never be in the position where you could be lost in a fog, but when you are it's a comforting tool. Know how to use it—and use it before you need it.

There's no such animal as a dedicated fishing paddle. Considering the distances paddled and the conditions, you'll be more than happy with a slightly spooned molded-plastic blade and plastic-covered aluminum-shaft paddle. It will be a take-apart, with adjustment for paddling unfeathered or with the blades set at around 60 degrees. A step up would be a fairly small-bladed fiberglass paddle, also a take-apart. Figure on $80 to $100 for a good plastic model, $100 to $120 for a good fiberglass paddle. You can triple that for a superbly crafted composite paddle.

A GPS (global positioning system) receiver can tell you where you are on the water, can remember the spots you choose to return to, and can guide you to preselected destinations.

Take Care: Your sit-on-top is an amazingly seaworthy boat, but by any measure it still is a very small craft. Couple this with the fact that you're concentrating on fishing and not boating, and you can stumble into uncomfortable and potentially dangerous situations.

First, listen to the National Oceanic and Atmospheric Administration (NOAA) weather forecasts for your area and tie them in to as much local knowledge as you can absorb. We've all seen mirror-smooth waters churned into froth by advancing squall lines. Your best defense is not to launch in the first place; your second best is to sprint for the nearest shore as quickly as you can.

Think about winds. As a rule, the wind will blow from a cool area toward a warm one: When the sea is warmer than the land, you'll get an offshore breeze; when the land is warmer, you'll get an onshore breeze. An offshore breeze will tend to flatten wave action. You're liable to venture or drift farther than you suspect—and then be faced with a longer paddle into the teeth of the wind. It's always harder paddling upwind. An offshore breeze may increase the surf action, and it will make your landing harder just when you're tired and less careful.

When there's fog, stay on the beach. Sure, with electronics you can find your way back to your landing, but that's a game you don't want to play. If you've thought ahead, you can paddle a compass course back to the beach—if you know where the beach is. If you get confused, you'll be very hard to find. Even with a brightly colored sit-on-top, mast and flag, and bright paddles, you are difficult to see. If you're out and you see the fog start to build, it's beach time.

Dive! Dive! Dive!

Just as with fishermen, there are plenty of sit-on-top users who don't consider themselves to be boaters or even kayakers. Take, for example, divers. Everyone squirming into a wet suit, mask, and flippers in preparation for a swim to the bottom of the sea considers himself/herself to be a diver and not a paddler. And yet, if you think about it, the trip from the shore to the diving grounds is a perfect paddle, and today's lightweight, swift, and stable sit-on-top is the perfect dive vessel.

The sit-on-top or wash-deck design gives you excellent stability on the water, a wide range of storage options, and a platform that moves you to the diving grounds with unbelievable speed and comfort. Also, with just a few paddle strokes you're far from the madding crowd. Sit-on-top manufacturers know this well. While most general-purpose double sit-on-tops, and bigger singles, can be quickly rigged up for dive use, manufacturers have been quick to supply a wide range of dedicated dive platforms. Want to secure a tank (or rack of tanks), a buoyancy compensation device (BCD), or other gear (as well as the catch of the day) aboard? With a little forethought, you can easily lash your gear aboard a typical general-purpose sit-on-top. On the other hand, the loading and movement will be more convenient if you explore the options offered by specially molded tankwells and below-deck easy-access hatches.

If you're just as comfortable below the surface as on it, start by finding the brightest sit-on-top you can find. High-visibility colors make it easy for you to see your craft from below—and for others to see it on the surface.

Paddling out to the dive site will warm up any diver. When you're paddling, you're using your torso and arm muscles while saving your leg muscles for the swim. Put on your wet or dry suit before you launch. You're going to be more comfortable wearing your Farmer Johns and booties when you're actually paddling. Wet suit tops are designed for swimming, not paddling, and just don't allow you the freedom of motion the paddle demands. I've seen a fair number of dry suit divers paddle out with the top of their suit down, which makes for more comfortable paddling. A paddling jacket will keep water from trickling down into an open dry suit, as well as keep wind and weather off the skin of both wet- and dry-suit divers.

A stable and swift sit-on-top is the ideal dive tender, with plenty of room for one tank in the aft cargo well and another in the bow hatch. It's also easy for a swimmer to tow.

An unloaded sit-on-top bobs on the water and offers a dry ride. A loaded sit-on-top—with weights, tanks, and personal gear—is a different animal. It takes more paddling effort to get it up to cruising speed, but once you have it moving it has greater momentum. Where the empty sit-on-top will rise over small waves, the loaded one is more likely to punch through—and that means water over the bow and back to you. That's reason enough for the paddling jacket. At the same time the water is splashing you, it's sloshing over the hatches. If you remembered to cinch down the hatch straps and check your seals, you won't have a problem (or water gurgling belowdecks).

On my general-purpose tandem sit-on-top, an 80-cubic-foot aluminum tank will fit through the bow hatch. You might want to put a retrieval line on the tank before loading it below, just to make it easier to bring back out. I also have room for a pair of full tank/BCD setups in the well behind the rear paddler. Personal gear can go in the fore hatch, on top of the tank, with fins and anchor the last in and on top. They are the first two items you'll need at the dive site. A dive clip line makes it easier to clip your flashlight, camera, and other incidentals to your boat.

I like a large mesh bag to hold my wet suit top and fins, as well as my paddling jacket and hat at the site. It's easy to clip on deck and provides quick access.

The first thing you're going to do at the dive site is to anchor or tie up—unless you plan on towing your sit-on-top. Most sit-on-top paddlers who anchor will use one of the folding anchors for the convenience of stowing it. Make sure it's open and locked. Your anchor rode (line, if you prefer) should be at least three times as long as the water is deep. If it's twice as long (or less) as the water depth, your sit-on-top will tend to lift the anchor from the bottom rather than tug its flukes more securely into

A small, folding anchor will keep your sit-on-top from drifting while you're diving or fishing, and it's easy to stow when you're under way.

B A S I C   E S S E N T I A L S

the bottom. Don't skimp on the size of the anchor rode. A ¼-inch line may be strong enough, but it will also cut into your hands when you retrieve the anchor. Also, think about abrasion. A minor cut on a small line can reduce its strength below a safe level, while the same cut on a larger line is immaterial. To prevent tangling of the anchor rode, take a look at the throw bags sold in most whitewater shops. You just stuff the line back into the bag instead of coiling it, and it pays out easily and untangled.

The second thing you'll do at the dive site is slip on your fins. If you dangle your feet in the water, either straddling or sidesaddle, your sit-on-top will be more stable. Put on your top—wet suit or dry—open your hatch, and start unloading. Clip each item to the dive clip line and hang all of them in the water until you need them. Inflate the BCD and tether your tanks overboard. It's probably easier to put on your tanks in the water.

Double-check that your hatches are shut and secured and that your paddle is tethered with a paddle leash or snapped into paddle clips. Eyeball that your dive flag is on your mast and deployed, and off you go.

Another advantage of using your sit-on-top as a dive platform is that it's so easily towed by a swimmer. Use a longer towline than you first think you'll need. Your sit-on-top will bob with surface waves; a short line will tug at you, while a longer one will absorb the yanks and jerks.

When it comes to towing, though, human power is the only way to go. *NEVER* tow your sit-on-top behind a powerboat. Even at low speeds tremendous hydraulic forces are created that can break or collapse your kayak.

The Diving Basics

Whether or not you have a special dive sit-on-top, you're going to want an assortment of special accessories. Start off with a dive flag and flag mount or mast, for safety. Add a grab line clear around the gunwales of your sit-on-top, both for a handhold when you're in the water and for tying off the assortment of objects you'll either want or have found. To make sure your sit-on-top is still there when you swim back (and for fishing), you'll need a slightly heavier folding anchor and an anchor rode from three to seven times as long as the water is deep. Fill the hull with flotation bags and dry bags to store the gear and clothing you want to protect from the dribbles and damp.

Whitewater Extras

A whitewater sit-on-top is one of the best ways to play in the froth or foam of a tumbling river. Make sure your sit-on-top has some form of thigh/knee brace that allows you to hold yourself in the cockpit as you paddle and brace, yet still lets you pop free by relaxing a muscle. A helmet is imperative (and in many locations required by law). Go with a real whitewater helmet rather than try to make do with a hockey or cycling helmet. They're designed for different impacts.

Protect the rest of your body as well. A neoprene wet suit or its fuzzy-rubber cousin will keep you warm but not dry. A dry suit will keep you dry but won't offer thermal protection. You'll probably want a light fleece or polypropylene liner for extra warmth. A wet suit will provide additional buoyancy and shelter from some of the bumps and bruises that you'll face while swimming (an essential part of learning!). If you have hatches, fill the interior of your sit-on-top with inflation bags. They'll add strength to your hull as well as make rescue/recovery easier in the unlikely event of a swamping. Grab handles at the bow and stern will make it easier to move your boat on land, and they are invaluable when you are assisting a swimmer.

For whitewater or surf trips, you'll need a helmet and some sort of thigh brace to help hold yourself firmly in place in your boat.

Surfing Extras

Start with all the options for a whitewater sit-on-top (whether or not you're paddling a model designed for the surf). If you're in a general-purpose sit-on-top—not a wave ski—you'll probably be more comfortable if you mount a backrest. A paddle leash—a cord—will keep you and your paddle together following an upsetting experience.

The Perfect Paddle

4

Think of your paddle as the transmission and driveshaft of your car: It takes the power from the engine (in a sit-on-top, that's you) and transmits it to the road (or with your sit-on-top, the water). You wouldn't expect a semi, a sports car, and a minivan to have the same transmission or the same wheels, right? Paddles are no different: A variety of lengths, blade shapes, and materials have been developed to meet the needs of whitewater paddlers, casual recreationists, and long-distance voyagers. You can find a general paddle that will do a bit of everything, but it will be less efficient, more tiring, and less durable than one designed for a specific type of paddling.

Does that mean you'll need a bagful of paddles, much like a golfer heading out on the greens? Nope. What it does mean is that as your paddling skills and interests increase, you're going to want one paddle for running a river and a different paddle for long-distance cruising.

Every paddle is a compromise among weight, durability, and cost. It's easy to balance any two of these, but it takes art and a high degree of craft to wrap all three into one package. Virtually all paddles, whitewater and touring, are made of four families of materials. The least expensive, and the heaviest, have thermo-molded plastic blades and aluminum shafts. For the price, they can be remarkably good. They can also be heavy, unresponsive clubs that will exhaust you within minutes. The most common blade and shaft material is fiberglass, which is a good compromise of weight, strength, and cost. Also, because so many are made, the purchasing paddler receives the economy of scale and the benefits of competition. Fiberglass paddles will stand up to being banged on, rocked, stepped on, scuffed, and used to push off from a beach, and they won't scuttle your wallet. Carbon fiber, graphite, and other exotic composites are light and strong, but the raw materials are expensive and it

Paddles come in all shapes, sizes, weights, lengths, and blade styles. The paddle on the right is a whitewater paddle; the other four are touring paddles.

takes skill to produce a quality product with them. You might pay three times as much for a carbon-fiber paddle as you would for fiberglass, and because of that you'll be less likely to bash one around in whitewater or on an ocean beach. On the other hand, it sure is sweet to paddle those light blades on an extended trip in deep water. Wood is a craftsman's dream and will shape into a truly beautiful paddle. Unfortunately, you'll also pay dearly for that work of art when you buy it, and in time as you sand, revarnish, and maintain it. If they weren't so attractive and didn't feel so good in your hand, you'd be tempted to dismiss wood paddles— but because of those two pluses you just can't.

What should you look for in a touring-type paddle for your sit-on-top? Start by examining the blade. The blade itself is going to be relatively long and light, with corners that are soft and rounded. Every fraction of an ounce on the end of that blade is multiplied many times by the length of the shaft. Since you'll swing the paddle thousands of times in a paddling day, blade weight is a *very* significant factor.

The blade is slightly cupped so that when you insert it into the water it will stay where you put it. The whole idea of paddling is to stick your paddle into thick and high-resistance water and to slide your sit-on-top

This graphite asymmetrical touring paddle with its cupped blade balances your power on both sides of the shaft and is very stable in the water.

up to the paddle. The cupped power face makes the blade more stable as you pull on it.

Most enthusiast-quality paddle blades are asymmetrical: The top half of the blade extends a little farther than the bottom half. When you insert the blade into the water at the normal paddling angle, though, the submerged surface area of the blade above the centerline will be the same as the surface area of the bottom half of the paddle.

Angles? That's the rule in today's paddles. A look at any paddle rack shows that most paddle blades are set at an angle to each other. Setting the blades at different angles is called "feathering." It started when flatwater racers realized they could gain a few thousandths of a second by offsetting their blades so that the upper blade would slice through the air edge first. For most recreational paddlers, it is easier to paddle directly into the wind with a feathered paddle—with the upper paddle blade slicing edge-first through the air. At the same time, if you're paddling across the wind with a feathered paddle, the uppermost blade presents its broad surface to the wind and the air will tug and push at it. About three-quarters of the kayak paddles made today are feathered, and at least three-quarters of them are feathered for right-hand control.

With a feathered kayak paddle, one hand always holds the shaft and rotates it so that the blades are in turn perpendicular to the water. It doesn't matter if you're right- or left-handed. Hold the paddle vertically in front of you, with the blade on the ground facing you. If the upper blade points to the right, it's a right-handed control blade; to the left, it's a left-handed blade.

Enthusiast-level paddles rarely have the blades set at a right angle to each other. To avoid carpal tunnel syndrome—which used to be called kayaker's wrist—blades are often offset around 60 degrees. Reducing the offset apparently reduces the potential for repetitive overrotation injury. However, below 45 degrees you'll lose most of the advantages of feathering.

Fortunately, you don't have to absolutely decide if you want a feathered or unfeathered paddle. A modern take-apart paddle has its shaft cut in half and joined at a sleeve or ferrule. You can choose to join the halves unfeathered or at a predetermined angle. Try it both ways and see what you like. A few paddles can be adjusted to any angle.

How much attention will you have to pay to the relative positions of the blades? Surprisingly little. Most good paddles have an oval rather than a round shaft, and in a matter of a few minutes your muscles learn blade position by feel. Not only that, the oval paddle shaft is much more comfortable to hold.

How long should a paddle be? To paraphrase Abraham Lincoln, long enough to reach the water. For an average-size paddler in an average-size sit-on-top, paddling with the center of the shaft at about navel level, a good starting length for a touring paddle is 220 to 226 centimeters. Most touring paddlers hold their paddles low, between their navel and their solar plexus, and they use a slower stroke cadence. Some paddlers hold their paddles higher, between the solar plexus and collarbone, and paddle with a faster stroke cadence. They'll use a slightly shorter paddle. The paddle held lower will enter the water at a lower angle, just to clear the gunwales of your sit-on-top. You'll thus need a longer paddle to get the blade into the water. If you hold your paddle higher, its angle will be steeper, and you won't need as long a shaft to reach the water. Holding the paddle higher generally results in a more efficient paddle stroke. You'll also see slightly larger paddle blades used by those who favor the higher paddle position.

Some paddle shafts are twisted through a number of angles. The idea, for skilled paddlers, is to keep the paddle blade at the most ergonomically efficient angle in the water with the least cocking and twisting of your wrists.

Most whitewater sit-on-top paddlers like feathered paddles. Most like oval shafts, most use drip rings, and there's an increasing trend toward asymmetrical blades. Most whitewater blades are wider and larger than touring blades. Blade tips are reinforced because they get bashed on rocks and the bottom, and stouter blades are heavier. Single-piece shafts are more common. Paddle lengths are shorter. For an average paddler, the average length is around 206 centimeters.

Know your paddling desires and your involvement before you start writing checks for a new paddle. A $400 carbon-fiber touring paddle is a waste of money if you want to drift around a bass pond. A plastic blade and aluminum shaft paddle will mean a lot more effort on a long island-hopping voyage. Knowing, really knowing, how and where you want to paddle is your best guide to the paddle you'll really want.

The Essential Accessories

5

I f you're aboard your sit-on-top and floating on navigable waters—
that's lawyer talk for just about any water in North America—you are
required by federal law to have a wearable personal flotation device
aboard for each person, and you must have a whistle or other sound-
making device. Lights are required when it's dark. On top of this, local
governments can and often do set a whole list of other standards and
rules as to what you must have and when, and what licenses and
regulations you must follow. In other words, check with your state
Boating Law Administrator (every state has one, usually in its Parks and
Recreation or Natural Resources Department) before you go.

You should also carry, as a matter of your own safety and comfort, a
pump and sponge to remove water from inside your sit-on-top; float bags
(inflatable bags placed inside your sit-on-top's hull for additional buoyancy and strength); duct tape for emergency patching; a throw line for
helping someone else or yourself; and a first-aid kit, along with the
knowledge of how to use it.

Tuck away a Space Blanket for protection from sun, wind, and
hypothermia—as an alternative, a big plastic garbage sack works almost
as well—quick-energy food for when your personal fuel tank hits zero,
and a good supply of drinking water. Eat before you are hungry; drink
before you're thirsty. It is very, very easy to become dehydrated on the
water!

Your PFD

It's a brilliant, beautiful day and you're about to launch your sit-on-top for a quick paddle on a sheltered little bay. But wait a moment—don't you feel kind of naked?

In the first place, Uncle Sam says you must have a wearable personal flotation device aboard for every person on your sit-on-top. In the second place, many state, county, or other local laws demand that you wear your PFD anytime you're afloat. In the third, and most important, place, Mother Nature says you're foolish if you venture out on her waters without the support of your PFD, regardless whether local laws call for it.

The Coast Guard, which sets federal boating rules, defines five different classes of approved flotation devices. Type I is the big and bulky offshore life jacket that offers lots of flotation but is not comfortable for paddling. Type II is the familiar "horsecollar" with ties in the front and a waist belt. Type III is the vestlike flotation device most paddlers wear, and for that matter what probably the majority of all recreational boaters wear. It's light, comfortable, and stylish and gives you both freedom of action and adequate protection in nearshore waters, rivers, and other areas where rescue is near if you have a problem. Type V is a special-purpose PFD, normally a pull-over flotation device for competition or an inflatable model. Type IV devices, boat cushions and throw rings, are not approved for sit-on-tops—or any other kayak.

Take a look at any rack of personal flotation devices in a modern water sports shop and you'll be dazzled by the vast array of products available. Before you're too dazzled, though, let's separate out what today's sit-on-top paddler really needs and what might be nice to have along.

Most sit-on-top paddlers will swear by Type III PFDs. They're comfortable, they provide an adequate amount of support in the water, and they offer you a full range of paddling motion. Most Type III PFDs are waist-length with a belt cinching them tight at the bottom. A smaller number have a short "skirt" of flotation extending down from the waist. Because of your paddling position and backrest, a waist-length PFD is going to be more comfortable than a longer model. The label may tell you that a particular PFD is for CANOEING/KAYAKING (or similar words), or identify it as GENERAL PURPOSE. The canoeing/kayaking PFDs are shaped to allow a full range of paddling motions and stay in the most comfortable position during all the twists and contortions you'll attempt while on your sit-on-top.

Most PFDs are made of panels: one for the back, one for each side of the zipper in front. Some are made with a number of vertical "tubes" of flotation. Which you choose is a matter of personal preference and style—try both styles on, and find the one that fits you the best.

Again, most of the PFDs on the rack have a zipper right down the middle of the front. And that works super well. A smaller number have a solid front panel and a zipper on the side under one arm. A lot of paddlers find the side-entry PFDs more comfortable.

The better manufacturers make PFD models for both men and women. If you're going to wear one for a day on the water, you deserve comfort!

If you read the tag on a PFD, you'll see that a Type III offers a minimum of fifteen and a half pounds of flotation. Don't start comparing your weight to that number. When in the water, the average adult male requires between seven and twelve pounds of flotation to keep his head comfortably above water.

PFDs come in a variety of styles and with an amazing array of features. What's important is to find one that fits you properly—and remember to wear it whenever you're on the water.

You may well see another set of numbers—for example, FOR OVER 90 POUNDS. That has nothing to do with the flotation a PFD offers. Instead, it reflects the size of the person for whom it was designed. An ADULT PFD is for someone who weighs more than ninety pounds; a YOUTH is for someone who weighs fifty to ninety pounds. You may also see SMALL, MEDIUM, LARGE, and EXTRA LARGE. A YOUTH is also for a person with a 25- to 29-inch chest, an ADULT LARGE is for a person with a 43- to 45-inch chest, and an ADULT EXTRA LARGE is for a person with a 46- to 50-inch chest.

How do you know if a PFD fits you? Put it on over your regular paddling clothes, snug down the compression straps under each armhole and the waist strap comfortably, and sit on the floor in your paddling position. Have a friend stand over you and attempt to lift your PFD by the shoulder straps. If the PFD slips up, it's the wrong size or improperly adjusted. If you're raised up, the PFD fits.

The basic PFD is designed to keep a conscious person's head above water. Basic works, but look at some of the options available to make your sit-on-top paddling more friendly—like a small pocket. Lip balm, sunscreen, a candy bar, a folding knife—you'll carry a pocketful of goodies with you as you paddle. The pocket should be closed by a zipper or with a flap and a hook-and-loop patch, because when you swim you're bound to shed any loose object you really want to keep. Look inside the pocket for a loop of cord, perfect for tying off your keys.

Reflective patches on your shoulder straps or across the back will make you much easier to see, no small comfort when powerboats are whizzing about at the end of the day. Look for another, easily accessible loop to secure your whistle lanyard. Another option you'll appreciate is a four-way lash tab, a great place to hook on a knife or a light.

Find a PFD that's comfortable, find a PFD that fits, and when you're on the water, wear it.

Dress for
Excess

J ust about all paddlers, at some time in their lives, dream of drifting along off the white sand beach of a tropical island, basking (in the bare minimum before nothing) in the delightful collision of a warm sun and a gentle sea breeze.

And now for the reality check. Your sit-on-top is the most exposed of all small craft that take to the waters, and you have to shelter yourself from the sun, cold, wind, and water. Fortunately, with today's technical clothing, it's easy.

Let's start in the middle. In balmy weather you're going to be most comfortable in river shorts, guide shorts, or similarly baggy shorts. They'll dry quickly, chafing is limited, they offer your legs and back some abrasion protection from your sit-on-top, and they'll have both a mesh liner for added protection and mesh pockets for quick water drainage. Cutoff jeans will be binding, and once wet, they will stay damp forever. Most "bathing" or "swim" suits are more style than substance. You'll chafe wherever bare skin contacts your sit-on-top or seat, the seams will wear on your water-softened skin, and they'll ride up into tender areas.

If the water gets a tad colder, consider wearing neoprene shorts that fall just above the knee. Some may have Lycra front panels. These mini wet suits will add a fair degree of warmth and protection without binding on you. You'll find them at paddle sports shops (especially those haunted by the competitive set), surf shops, and some dive shops.

Top off your shorts with a synthetic fabric T-shirt, again looking for a quick-drying and nonbinding fit from a manufacturer that understands paddle sports. Cotton tees will soon get and stay soggy.

Most of us understand cold but forget about the impact of sunlight. If you're a shorts person, swab down your legs (as well as arms, ears, and face) with a good sunblock. You're going to be wet, so your best place to find the block you want is at a dive shop or at a good paddle sports store with a competitive clientele. A super sunblock that washes off is useless.

There are a few clothing manufacturers around—Ex Officio is one—that fabricate shirts from sun-impervious material. Look for one that is long-sleeved, with a collar that will button up high around your neck.

On top of everything wear a cap or hat with a long bill to protect your eyes and head. If you're wearing a cap, look for one with a Foreign Legion skirt that will cover your neck and ears. I've seen unwary paddlers burn and scorch in just a few hours on a cloudy day, until the tops of their ears blister, break, and scab over. A chinstrap will keep the wind from snatching your hat away. If it's cold, your cap is going to provide a substantial amount of insulation for the body part that radiates the most heat. Sunglasses, even on a cloudy day, are far more than a fashion item—they are a necessity if you don't want cold compresses on your face and a maximum dose of headache medicine later on that day. A safety strap will keep them on your head.

Slather that sunblock on your hands, and remember lip protection. The sun is going to reflect off the water and bite you in unexpected places. More than a few of my paddling friends carry along fingerless gloves or pogies—a sort of mitten that wraps around the paddle shaft and engulfs your hands—for cooler days and wind protection.

Barefoot is way cool when you're sitting on the manicured grass at a public park. When you're kayaking, however, this is another case where fantasy and reality just don't jibe. The wind on your toes feels nice until your feet are a little soft from immersion and your heels start to chafe. Or you walk across that tropic beach and discover that the sun makes sand hot. Or you hobble across a rocky beach, hopping around broken glass. Or . . . hey, you get the picture.

The best line of defense is a good pair of river sandals. They provide plenty of support and protection for the soles of your feet (as well as tender heels and sides), and they don't mind getting wet in the slightest. Paddling guides live in a wet environment and demand high levels of protection. Seek out what the guides wear, and copy that.

If the temperature drops just a bit, slip on a pair of breathable, waterproof socks under your sandals. Mine are above the ankle, and I can splash around in the foam and keep my feet dry. I usually wear a pair of lightweight synthetic socks under the waterproofs.

A note of caution: Some "river" sandals are cut with a really wide sole and heel and won't comfortably fit into the footwells on your sit-on-top. If the pair that fits your feet looks wide, test them on your boat before writing a check.

A paddling jacket with sealable cuffs and collar will keep you dry and comfortable but not restrict your movement. A long-billed and skirted cap (or wide-brimmed hat) will help protect your head from the sun.

I have, and wear, neoprene booties, but after a bit of vigorous pad-dling my feet start to sweat, and the booties stay damp for the rest of the day. Warm, yes, but damp. Water shoes—essentially sandals with a toe cover—are another option.

Tennies? Nope. They get wet and stay wet, and most will chafe—not to mention deteriorate fairly quickly.

As the temperature dips a bit more, slip into paddling pants and dry tops. These offer lots of protection from wind and water, and today's manufacturers design them to allow great freedom of motion. I've had waves break totally over me, and while I had to shake water from my face, the rest of me stayed dry and comfortable. Look for a jacket with a sealable neck (either a flap or a gasket), sealable cuffs, and a long waist that snugs down. Dry pants and a dry top keep you—as the name implies—dry, not necessarily warm. Some paddlers like a synthetic polypropylene "union suit" to keep warm. I find polypro tights and a l-o-n-g polypro top with a zipper that converts the neck from a V to a tur-tle to be the most comfortable.

A neoprene wet suit will keep you warm, sometimes too warm, but it does so at a price. You'll be double damp—from the water you're paddling over as well as the sweat you'll make. When the temperatures are low and immersion is a definite possibility, a wet suit may be your only choice, but realize that you'll spend the day damp. If you do go the neoprene route, go to a paddling shop and find the lightweight, thin neoprene rather than the heavier kind used by most divers. Neoprene's close cousin, "fuzzy" rubber, offers the thermal protection of neoprene with additional comfort, but at the cost of less abrasion resistance.

What's the best idea? Plan for the worst possible conditions, and expect the very best. Layering—multiple light clothing layers, each designed for a specific task or condition—works better than one heavy, all-purpose layer. That way you can shed or add as the day demands, protecting your tender skin from sun, wind, waves, rain, heat, and chill.

Getting to the Water

Some lucky people live on the shores of the most fascinating waters of the world and can launch from the beach for new adventures every day. In the real world, though, you must haul your sit-on-top from a few blocks to many miles before you can explore the variety of waters open to you.

The easiest way to transport a sit-on-top is on a roof rack atop your vehicle. A roof rack is a pair of parallel bars extending crosswise over your roof, supported at each end by pillars or clips that attach to your vehicle. Cradles (or saddles) secure to the crossbars and support the hull. Stackers will hold your sit-on-top, as will vertical supports that hold your sit-on-top on edge. There are all kinds of attachments, including wheeled supports rather than cradles, that allow you to roll your sit-on-top into position, as well as offset extenders that make it easier to lift your sit-on-top onto the rack. Yakima and Thule set the standards for strength, versatility, and durability, but don't write off other manufacturers until you shop and compare. Unfortunately, many of the rails permanently mounted on some vehicles are all flash and no strength—and are held in place with no more than a few sheet-metal screws. Check with the vehicle's manufacturer as to the carrying capacity of any built-in rail system. As you drive, the wind can generate tremendous lifting and twisting forces on your sit-on-top, and you wouldn't want it to rip the rails out of your vehicle's roof!

The rack—the crossbars—can be used all by itself. The crossbars should be padded, because prolonged time on bare racks could dent your sit-on-top. Start by placing your sit-on-top upside down on the paddled bars, centering it over the bars. Strap the sit-on-top in place with ropes or straps across the hull at each crossbar. If your sit-on-top has scupper holes (drain holes in the cockpit and footwells), thread the straps through them. Tie the straps snugly, but don't really reef down on them—too ambitious a tug could dent your sit-on-top. Tie bow and stern lines to your bumpers. Again, don't put a huge amount of tension on these lines, because you can place excessive stress on your sit-on-top right at the crossbars. Don't forget to secure those bow and stern lines. More than one unhappy boater has left a stern line dangling and then backed over it—crumpling the hull at the rack.

Soft pads are, as the name suggests, simply a set of soft foam pads placed on the roof of your car to support your sit-on-top. They're cheap, they work, and while they are not as effective or efficient as a crossbar system, they're certainly easy to store when not in use. Follow the directions that come with the pads for mounting them atop your vehicle, then place your sit-on-top upside down on them. Run straps over the hull (and through the scupper holes, if available) and through your vehicle windows or doors. Don't overtighten—you could dent your sit-on-top or vehicle roof. Secure bow and stern lines to your bumpers and you're in business.

Moving your sit-on-top to new waters? If you don't have a permanent rack (the most convenient option), a couple of blocks of foam and some straps to fasten your sit-on-top to the car will work just fine.

With any carrying system, stop periodically and make sure no lines have started to work loose.

If you're using a roof rack system, check it periodically for rust, damage, and wear. While most of us leave them on our vehicles year-round, prudence demands that we care for the racks.

You don't need a car to transport your sit-on-top. There are a variety of carts available that will support your craft and allow you to roll it on pavement, on grass, or over a beach. The Farrington Chariot even has an extended tongue that allows you to tow your sit-on-top behind your bicycle.

Never tow your sit-on-top behind a powerboat. It's a matter of destructive physics. Your sit-on-top's displacement hull will literally have its stern pulled deeper in the water if you try to tow it. The hydraulic effect of the sinking stern, the great drag, and the rising bow will put catastrophic stress on the hull about a quarter of the way back from the bow.

If you have a long way to carry your sit-on-top from the car to the water, consider using a cart.

Off-Season
Storage

W hen it comes time to park your plastic sit-on-top for a day or a season, store it on edge, upside down, standing, or hanging. *Never* just leave it bottom-side down, for this could damage or distort the keel and affect the way your sit-on-top glides or tracks.

If you're going to hang your sit-on-top, use three or four wide straps and run them around the outside of the hull near the cockpit(s). On a double, use at least a pair of straps at each cockpit. Narrow cords may be strong enough to support the weight of your sit-on-top, but concentrating the hull's weight on those cords could potentially distort or crease the hull. Don't attempt to hang your sit-on-top from the scuppers or drain holes in the cockpit and footwells. Most don't offer the structural strength of a wide strap around the hull, and you may well distort or damage the holes.

Protect your sit-on-top from the sun. Sure, every manufacturer I know blends UV-inhibitors into the polyethylene when it molds a plastic hull; still, extended exposure to the sun can bleach the hull color and, in the worst case, can make the hull itself brittle. I know plastic sit-on-tops old enough to vote that are still colorful and in super shape, so perhaps this advice is in the wear-both-belt-and-suspenders class. But those sit-on-tops were stored properly, were kept clean, and had their hulls waxed several times a season as well as when put up for a winter's rest. Store your sit-on-top indoors or under a tarp that allows air movement. If you're storing your sit-on-top outside, build a little frame to shape the tarp and to protect it from the weight of the snow.

The manufacturer used heat to shape the plastic in your sit-on-top's hull. Polyethylene becomes soft at about 100 degrees and can lose its memory at 135 degrees. Polyethylene becomes brittle at –40, so if you shiver through cold winters you might want to store your sit-on-top in a protected area.

At the very least, rinse your sit-on-top after each paddle. It sure won't hurt to scrub it down with warm water and a mild detergent (you don't need an abrasive cleaner, which will just scratch up the finish anyway) periodically. The most significant long-term damage to your sit-on-top comes from prolonged exposure to the sun. Store your sit-on-top inside, or keep it covered.

Lastly, don't get in the habit of putting away your sit-on-top by the calendar and leaving it all winter. Some of the nicest paddling can come on a clear winter day and a patch of open water. Sure, you'll have to dress for the weather, but both you and your sit-on-top will appreciate the trip.

Self-Rescues

I f you watch sit-on-top paddlers for even a short time, you'll recognize that there are two broad groups: those working to enhance their paddling skills and those paddling with the intention of never getting their hair wet. Paddlers working to enhance their skills explore just how far they can lean a boat before losing stability; they accelerate and turn and come to sliding stops. In other words, they play. And yes, by testing the boundaries of their skills and their boats, they occasionally flop on over. In doing so they learn what they can do in a particular situation, and by knowing the far shores of their abilities, they are far less likely to panic or do a stupid thing if the world goes a bit wrong.

More conservative paddlers sit quietly in the middle of the kayak, arms held in, hands close together on the paddle, paddling with little precise strokes and never daring the potential of the kayak or the water. They'll never know just what the combination of their skills and the kayak design can accomplish or just how their muscles should react in an unexpectedly challenging situation—and I suspect they'll never know just how much fun you can have on a sit-on-top. At the take-out, sitting on a beach, conservative paddlers may boast that they haven't had to swim, that they haven't lost it, for years. If you listen closely, they're really confessing that they approach the water with timidity rather than respect.

If you ain't swimmin', you ain't learnin'.

If you know why you transmogrified from a paddler to a swimmer, you've enhanced your paddling skills. If you don't have a clue, then it's time to take a seat on the beach and evaluate your paddling knowledge.

Let's say you do flop over. How are you going to get to the beach?

You have three choices. You can scramble back aboard your kayak, a maneuver that takes only a few practiced seconds. If your kayak is so rigged, you can easily Eskimo-roll it back upright. Or you can swim to the shore, towing (or at least you should be) your kayak.

In a traditional kayak, after you flop over you have but two choices: roll up or swim. Once you're out of the traditional kayak it is extremely difficult—even for a trained and skilled paddler—to reboard. Hundreds of pounds of water are sloshing about inside, making the kayak very unstable, and you're going to have to balance your boat in the conditions that put you over in the first place while also attempting to remove the water.

If you flop your sit-on-top, the worst you're going to face is a few pints of water on the seat and in the footwells.

There are as many ways of scrambling back aboard your sit-on-top as there are paddlers, and most of them work pretty well. The easiest I've seen is the "Bellybutton, Backside, and Feet" technique, which was first spelled out to me by Mark Olson, a representative for Ocean Kayak.

If the boat is upside down, you'll have to flip it upright. To accomplish this, reach across about the midpoint of the boat's bottom and grab the far side. Bring your knees up and onto the bottom of the boat. Lean back, and the kayak will roll over. You'll flop clear, but the kayak may land on your legs. It's a surprise.

Position yourself so that your head is at about the midpoint of your kayak's cockpit area, so that you're floating on your stomach facing the kayak. Let your feet float to the surface.

Reach over the top of your kayak to the far gunwale and then swim up and on your kayak—kicking with your feet and pulling with your arms until your belly button is just across the centerline of your kayak. Your belly should be midway between the seat and the footwells.

Next, roll over on your backside toward the seat so that your backside ends up in the seat. You're facing the sky. Sit up, swing your feet into the footwells, and you're ready to go.

You'll struggle the first time, but that's to be expected when trying something new. With a few practice runs in sheltered water, you'll be able to swing aboard in five to ten seconds. When you're comfortable, the third or fourth time you try it, keep your paddle in your hand as you swing aboard. I've seen a few folks tuck their paddle under a deck strap; while that works, I'd rather have mine in hand. Another option, more common on cruising/touring kayaks, is the use of a paddle leash securing your paddle to your boat.

The Eskimo Roll

Rolling a kayak is a lot like riding a bicycle—someone can tell you how to do it, but it's awfully hard to learn from the pages of a book. Still, add a few minutes in the water with a skilled instructor and you'll have all the

If you're planning on doing any Eskimo rolling with your sit-on-top, you'll need thigh straps or some type of retention system to keep yourself from falling out.

mechanics down pat. Perfection, and a bombproof roll, comes only with practice.

In a rapid or in the surf zone, a roll is the quickest way to regain control of your kayak. That said, it takes practice, and you'd better have a solid reboarding technique as a precaution in case you miss your roll.

First of all, let's take a look at your sit-on-top. If you have just a divot for your backside and wells for your heels, an Eskimo roll won't work. You're just going to fall out of the kayak when inverted.

You need some sort of retention system. Most common are straps on each gunwale, under which you can place your knees/thighs. The pressure between your feet in the footwells and the straps will hold you in the kayak, and all you have to do to come clear is simply relax your feet and knees. A simple and elegant system. Some sit-on-tops have a contoured central pillar between your thighs; clamp your legs together, and you can hold yourself to the pillar. The downside is that if you learned to paddle in a conventional kayak, you'll want to force your legs out to lock into the thigh braces under the cockpit rim. That will release you from a pillar system, and you'll float free. If the sit-on-top is your first boat and your instructor understands this, you won't have a problem.

The third alternative is very effective, and yet I'm hesitant to use it. Some very experienced paddlers like car- or airplane-type waist belts. These offer great support, keep you in the proper paddling position, and provide tremendous stability. But you have to have the presence of mind to reach down with one hand and release the buckle when you want to be free of the boat. In a shallow river or surging toward a shelving beach while upside down, I'd just as soon relax my knees and abandon ship when my roll isn't working.

The most common kind of kayak roll is called the C-to-C roll, because your body curves to one side in a C as you start and ends up curved into a C on the other side. It's the easiest to teach. The roll is only going to work, though, when you have thigh straps, a center post, or a similar way of stabilizing yourself on your sit-on-top.

If you and your kayak are upside down in the water, start your roll by positioning your paddle along the outside seam of your kayak. The power face of the active blade should be facing down. Sweep the blade out at a right angle to your kayak. You'll feel air on the knuckles of your active blade hand, and your nonactive elbow should be touching the bottom of your kayak. Your torso is now forming a C toward your nonactive side. Once you're upside down, relax for a moment and let your adrenaline jag drain away. Brace up by moving your body, from your hips to your head, until it forms a C toward your active side. Hold your elbows close to your body to prevent stress on your shoulders. As the boat rotates back to right-side up, your head will be the last thing to leave the water.

With practice and someone to help you in the water, your muscles will learn the motions.

What About Swimming?

Swimming with an undamaged sit-on-top is easy, but it's different from swimming with a swamped canoe or traditional kayak. You're not trying to guide hundreds of pounds of water sloshing around the inside of the hull. However, you're in a current (water) environment while your sit-on-top is being pushed around by wind and wave action. In a wind your sit-on-top can be blown away from you—possibly faster than you can swim. While you're being moved by a current, your sit-on-top can be bounced around by waves.

The first rule is to be always upcurrent from your sit-on-top. Don't get trapped between your boat and an immovable object. Second, if possible, also try to stay upwind of your sit-on-top. Both may not be possible.

You'll find it surprisingly easy—relatively speaking—to tow your sit-on-top while swimming, but only if you remember that you're being acted upon by two or more different forces that may not be coming from the same direction. You're subject to waves, currents, and wind. You may not be able to swim directly against the current or against the wind, and

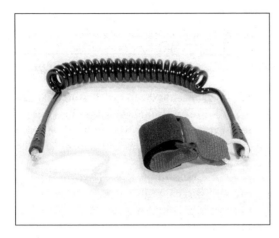

Misplacing your paddle ranges from embarrassing at best to a disaster at worst. A paddle leash will keep you connected to your power source.

wave action only complicates matters. Remember that you may have to circumvent or overcome all three forces, not just one of them, to swim to a safe haven.

A note about paddle leashes: A paddle leash is a strap that ties your paddle to your sit-on-top and is long enough to allow you full paddling freedom. The advantage is that you won't drop your paddle and see it drift away from your sit-on-top—or, even worse, not see it as it drifts away. The disadvantage is that a paddle can be a powerful swimming aid, and if you're upset and separated from your sit-on-top, you have also lost contact with your paddle.

Basic Paddling Strokes

Making your sit-on-top go is about the easiest thing you'll ever do in a boat on the water. Making it go where you want with the least expenditure of effort takes a little practice, but that's a win-win situation. Being on the water is a reward in and of itself, and gaining skill and expertise with each stroke is the frosting on a very good cake.

Listen to sit-on-top paddlers and you'll hear the names of dozens of paddle strokes bandied about. But before you get overwhelmed, just look at your paddle blade. It has two faces, a front and a back. And when you get down to basics, that's all the strokes you can use—one with the front or power face, and the other with the back of the blade.

Start by sitting up straight in your sit-on-top, with your feet comfortably pressed against the footwells and your back supported at the backband or seat. Reach just past your toes with a paddle blade—without leaning forward—and insert the blade in the water as you fully extend your arm (like you're poking something with a spear). Keep that arm extended, and then push out and forward with your other arm. Thrust forward with your upper arm by rotating your torso. The blade in the water will end up just behind your hip. Don't allow your upper hand to rise up higher than about your chin or nose. As the blade in the water passes your hip, bend your elbow to lift the blade from the water. The other blade is now over the centerline of your sit-on-top, your upper arm is extended, and you're in the perfect position to start your next stroke.

By keeping your arms extended and rotating your torso, you're capitalizing on the large muscle groups of your torso rather than relying on the smaller muscles of your arms.

When paddling forward, insert your paddle in the water near your feet and close to the side of your sit-on-top.

Why don't you want the paddle blade to pass beyond your hip? Because the blade is vertical in the water at that point. Past there you're actually lifting the blade, along with a load of water, and that just wastes your effort and muscle.

Most new paddlers think of pulling the paddle through the water. The reality is that you stick your paddle into the water and pull yourself up to where the blade is held immobile.

Turning

That's good for going ahead, but what about when *ahead* isn't where you want to go?

Start with the same stroke and modify it a bit. Instead of planting your paddle blade and pulling yourself up to it, stick the blade into the water and, while keeping the blade near the surface, swing it in an arc from the bow to amidships—straight out to the side from your cockpit. You'll feel as if you're pushing the paddle out from the bow, but what you're doing is pushing the bow away from the paddle.

If your paddle is near the surface and straight out from your hip, you can continue the stroke to pull the stern of your sit-on-top toward the paddle. It's a continuation of the turning motion.

The "sweep" stroke does another thing for you. If during the stroke you rotate the upper edge of your paddle blade slightly backward, in the direction of the stroke, the paddle will tend to rise to the surface. By matching the "lift" from your paddle with your own weight, you create a very stable righting motion that will support you if your sit-on-top is tilted to the side.

Tilt is a good thing. You can constantly adjust your course by sweep strokes on one side and the other, but every bit of correction takes away from your go-ahead effort.

Sit comfortably in your sit-on-top, with your knees tucked under your knee straps if you have them, your feet snugly in the footwells, and your back against your backband or seat. Keep your upper body vertical; move from just the waist down to rock your sit-on-top from side to side. You'll find you do this by raising one knee and pressing down with the other cheek.

Now take a few paddle strokes to start gliding through the water. Once you're in motion, lift your left knee and put more weight on your right cheek—but as you lean the boat, keep your upper body vertical. Your sit-on-top will turn in a graceful arc to the left.

Try it again by lifting your right knee, and your sit-on-top will turn to the right. You've just turned by using a J-lean.

Your center of gravity is directly over the sit-on-top's center of buoyancy when you are at rest or paddling normally. That's one reason the sit-on-top is so stable. If you leaned by moving your shoulders to the left (or right), you'd be rocking over like a bell buoy. The farther you lean, the farther your center of gravity moves from your center of buoyancy—and you'll learn the critical point in the middle of a great splash.

Knee lifts and tilting your sit-on-top give you subtle control over your direction. Couple the J-lean with a sweep stroke, and you stabilize your sit-on-top while increasing the sharpness of the turn.

Work on that J-lean. With it, you can rock with the waves and wakes that come from your side. By just letting your sit-on-top move underneath you, without fighting it or freezing up, you'll be a far more relaxed and efficient paddler.

If you're at rest and want to abruptly change your heading, you can sweep ahead on one side, or you can start a sweep stroke at the stern and reverse its motion. Either action will pivot your sit-on-top around its center.

Bracing

What happens if you lean beyond your center of balance? Without preparation, you'll have a perfect opportunity to practice reboarding. With preparation, you can regain stability with just a flick of the wrist.

Your easy options are the bracing strokes. The low brace has your wrists and palms atop the paddle shaft; the high brace has your palms and wrists underneath the paddle shaft. In one case the paddle is lower than your palms; in the other, it's higher. The low brace has the paddle shaft at the level of your navel; the high brace, no higher than your shoulders.

Let's try a low brace. Get comfortable on your sit-on-top, lower your paddle to around your navel, and bring your upper arm (on the side to which you're going to brace) just about straight out from your shoulder.

The low brace is a quick stabilizing move with your power applied to the back of the paddle blade. It's "low" because the paddle shaft is lower than your wrists.

Your upper arm and forearm will make somewhat of a right angle. Extend your paddle over the water, with the power side of the blade facing up and horizontal, and "punch" at the water with the back face of the blade. Don't push deeply into the water; just try for a vigorous splash. You'll feel a momentary support, just enough for you to unweight your knee on that side and weight your other-side cheek. You won't support yourself for long, but you will be able to push off to regain your equilibrium. Paddlers call this a hip flick or knee lift, and it's the same move you used in the J-lean to turn.

The high brace also restores your equilibrium, but it does so with the power face of your paddle. Center yourself on your sit-on-top and raise your paddle until it's at the level of and parallel to your shoulders. The high brace is performed with the paddle blade horizontal to the water, power-side down. Extend the paddle until your offside hand is at your shoulder and the paddle blade is just at the surface of the water. A sharp downward pull will freeze the paddle blade in the water, and with the same hip flick and unweighting-weighting move described above, you can quickly scoot your sit-on-top back to vertical.

Don't lift your paddle high over your head while doing this stroke. Your shoulders aren't designed to cope with that level of stress when they're so extended. You could well learn firsthand just how uncomfortable reducing a dislocated shoulder can be!

Now, obviously, either of these bracing strokes is going to support you for only a moment—and in most cases that's quite enough. You can, though, greatly and almost indefinitely extend the support from either stroke.

Slap the water just as you practiced in the low brace and, with the paddle extending straight out from your sit-on-top, slightly rotate the paddle shaft so that the edge of the blade toward the bow is angled slightly upward. Then reverse-sweep the paddle toward the bow. The paddle blade will attempt to rise in the water, just as your hand does when you're pretending like it's an airplane out a car window. You'll be surprised how much support it gives. You can reverse the tilt of the blade so that the aft edge is tilted up, and sweep the blade toward the stern to increase the duration of the support. How long can you keep it up? How strong are you? If you rotate the blade the wrong way and sweep, the paddle will dive; instead of being supported, you'll have the opportunity to practice reboarding.

Try the same series of motions with your high brace. You'll find you can hang off your paddle—with practice—for a long time with much of your weight over the side of your sit-on-top and over the water.

In either case you'll soon be able to balance your sit-on-top with the

The high brace is a stabilizing stroke with your power applied to the power face or front of the paddle blade. It's "high" because the paddle shaft is higher than your wrists.

deck nearly vertical and a lot of your weight on the blade. And it's not just a trick to impress nonpaddling friends. If you ever need to stabilize your sit-on-top in an immediate, critical situation, you'll be able to do so.

With the basic high brace, you're able to move your sit-on-top sideways in the water. Start with a low-impact high brace, and instead of just balancing on the blade for a moment, pull the blade from where you inserted

Make sure you've practiced your bracing and steering skills before you take on the surf.

it—3 feet or so from the side of your sit-on-top—to within a foot of your gunwale. Don't come in too close, because you can overrun your blade and trip over it. When doing this draw stroke, keep your boat as flat on the water as you can. You want to slide the hull sideways, not let it dig in.

One of the neat things about kayaking is that you have a blade on each side of the sit-on-top. Practice your leans, sweeps, braces, and draws on both sides until you really don't have to think about how to do each one.

Rivers from Mild to Wild

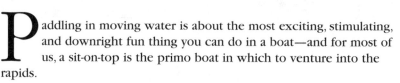

Paddling in moving water is about the most exciting, stimulating, and downright fun thing you can do in a boat—and for most of us, a sit-on-top is the primo boat in which to venture into the rapids.

First of all, let me lay out what I'll be talking about. A river is the splash and drainage of water that is poured somewhere up on the mountainside and rushes down to the level of all water that is the sea. Think

New scenery awaits you around every bend when you're paddling a river.

of it as the ultimate water slide. In the old days we used to scramble as far up on the hillside as we could and then launch our boats for a run down the middle of the river. The object was not to hit anything major. Somewhere along the line, someone realized that in any natural river there are any number of reverse currents and crosscurrents created by objects placed in the river for the express purpose of making it more fun. You can get a lot more technical and precise, but the reality is that an immobile object placed in moving water disrupts the passage of the flowing water. It splits the current, and the water flowing past leaves a hole or low spot. At some point past the obstacle, the water "realizes" there's a low spot behind the obstacle and flows into the depression. Since it "realizes" this at some distance downstream, the water flow curls around and flows back upstream to fill in the low spot.

If you want to be river literate, the reverse current behind an object is called an eddy; the line of demarcation between the different currents is an eddyline.

River boating today is the practice of riding the current in short hops downstream, while precisely turning into the eddies as a place to park while you rest or align yourself for the next downstream pitch.

To be a river paddler you have to be aware of the main downstream current, be aware of the eddies and crosscurrents within the overall current flow, and be able to instinctively react to the forces of the water on

Learn to read the water and watch the effects of the current along the riverbanks and other obstacles in the river.

your sit-on-top. It sounds far more complicated than it is, and a few hours spent playing on an easy river flow will introduce you to the art and craft. On the other hand, I've had the good fortune to paddle with some of the greatest whitewater kayakers in the world, and to a person they acknowledge that they learn a little more about paddling on every run down a river.

Easy river? Sure. Paddlers have created a scale of whitewater difficulty as a basis for comparing moving water. While it is somewhat subjective, provides a good indication of how difficult any particular stretch of whitewater may be at a defined water flow. Check out the scale in the River Difficulty sidebar.

I'm kicking around the term *whitewater*. Water can and will ooze along almost imperceptibly, its surface mirror-reflective and not a swirl marring its progress. On the other hand, it can fall in a sheet over a cliff. In between is the relatively swift passage of water through a somewhat obstructed passage, with the interruption and deflection of the current kicking the water up into waves, breaking waves, and frothy white spume. And that is whitewater.

The Appropriate Equipment

What kind of sit-on-top do you want for paddling whitewater? You want a hull that turns quickly and precisely, which means a short hull—8½ to 13 feet. All other things being equal, the longer a hull is, the more directionally stable it is. (That's another way of saying, "Long doesn't turn.") A smooth bottom will skid across rather than grab the water and will turn more easily. A hull that has its midships—the cockpit—bulging wider than the ends can be tilted on its side. This lifts the ends from the surface, effectively shortening the waterline length and allowing the hull to more easily pivot. A sharp, pointed bow will pearl-dive into a wave rather than having the buoyancy to ride over it. All things considered, that leaves you with a 9- to 11-foot hull with a smooth and keelless bottom, full ends for buoyancy, and a beam of 26 to 30 inches.

On top? For the most effective paddling, you want a low back support that you can lock yourself against with knee pressure; knee or thigh support that will hold you down against the seat (thigh straps over the knee on the outside of the cockpit are most common, while a center pedestal against which you can clamp your thighs works); and solid footwells in which you can lock your feet. This system holds you firmly on the sit-on-top for aggressive paddling and lets you bail out by just relaxing your knee muscles.

A toggle—a handle an inch or so in diameter and 4 inches or so long on a 3- to 4-inch strap—at the bow and stern offers a secure handhold

A Note of Caution

Of all the craft that play along the rivers, your sit-on-top is probably the easiest to paddle, the easiest to control, and arguably the most stable and maneuverable. What's the matter with that? It can be easy, all too easy, to venture into waters far greater than your paddling or river-reading skills allow. Learn to control your exuberance, and while testing the boundaries of your knowledge, be aware of your limitations and the immense power of even the most gentle river.

for carrying your sit-on-top on the land or holding on in the water. A fabric band loop might look practical, but it's possible to catch your hand in the loop if the sit-on-top is rotating in the water.

Most sit-on-tops will have a cork in one end, on the top of the bow or stern, sealing up the drain hole. You have to make sure that you have the cork and that it is attached to the hull with a sturdy lanyard. Sinking sort of ruins your whole day.

Many—not all, but many—sit-on-tops have one or more hatches that allow you access to the interior. First of all, that's good storage. Second, and even more important, that's a place to insert inflatable airtight bags. Blow them up and they will keep water out in the unlikely event that you pop a hatch, or the even lesser possibility that you gouge a nick in your hull.

In either case you should carry a small roll of duct tape for repairs (as well as for first aid, equipment repair, and keeping the water out of your lunch bag). If you think a roll is too big (it is), wrap a couple of turns of paper around a pencil for a core and carefully reroll a chunk of tape from the original to the new roll. If you do (heaven forbid) swamp or hole your sit-on-top, it's easy enough to empty the water through the drain hole. A good sponge helps in swamping out the last of the water.

Tricking you out is more important than clamping goodies onto your sit-on-top. Wear a PFD anytime you're on the water. There are all sorts of rude and completely justifiable names for those paddlers who lack the common sense to strap on the support they will eventually need. Swimming out of a capsized river kayak is not only common, it is a very positive affirmation that you're learning the limits of your sit-on-top.

If the water is frothy and white, the odds are that it is chilly. A wet or fuzzy-rubber suit offers you thermal protection—it will keep you warm—and it supplies a bit of buoyancy. Paddling pants and a paddling jacket will keep you more or less dry, although neither will shield you from the bite of cold water. It's a good idea to layer up a couple of polypro T-shirts, the outer one long-sleeved, and tights for thermal protection. I suggest something like Gates OvrSocks—waterproof yet breathable socks worn with sandals—or true water shoes with plenty of drainage.

Just as important as a PFD is a whitewater helmet. In shallow, rocky water and turbulent currents, the risk of bouncing your noggin off the bottom or a rock is real—and even more so with a sit-on-top. You're probably less likely to capsize a very stable sit-on-top than a conventional kayak, but it's correspondingly easier to abandon a sit-on-top than it is to disentangle yourself from the cockpit of a conventional kayak.

In very cold weather or water, you can wear pogies or mitts that wrap around the paddle shaft and keep the cold water off your hands.

Paddling the River

So you're all accoutred and standing on a riverbank. Now what?

Let's go paddling!

We'll start by launching the sit-on-tops in a sheltered area out of the main flow of the river. The easiest way to board your sit-on-top is to straddle it, sit down, bring your feet into the footwells, and tuck your knees under the knee straps. Once in a while you won't have enough room (or the right conditions) to board this way. In this case bring your sit-on-top parallel to the shoreline, placing your paddle with one blade flat on the ground and the shaft at the other blade right behind the cockpit. Sit or squat next to the cockpit right in front of the paddle shaft, with your hands on the shaft. Lift yourself up, and shift your weight from the shoreside hand to the boatside hand as you put your boatside foot on your sit-on-top. With one foot in your boat, scoot sideways and lower yourself onto the seat. Bring your other foot aboard, and start paddling.

When you're on moving water, always be aware of the current's direction—and remember to lean downcurrent. If you lean into the current, the water can grab the edge of your sit-on-top, and you'll have the opportunity to practice self-rescue.

Your first move will be to cross the main flow of the river. If you tried to paddle straight across, the current would push you some distance downriver. Instead, angle across in a ferry. Keep your bow heading about 45 degrees into the current as you start. Paddle upstream as fast as the current is pushing you down, and at the same time move across the current. Just like you're on a rope. After a couple of times across the river, you'll see there's nothing magic about the 45-degree angle. Every river is different, so you'll change the angle and the power of your paddling to make the most efficient crossing.

Using your paddle as a brace is an effective way to board your sit-on-top.

River Difficulty

Paddlers have evolved a six-stage scale for rating the difficulty of paddling a particular stretch of river. Remember that difficulty will change with changes in water level.

Class I: Easy. Moving water with riffles and small waves. There are few obstacles, all obvious and easily missed with little training. The risk to swimmers is slight, and self-rescue is easy.

Class II: Novice. Straightforward rapids with wide, clear passages that are evident from the river without scouting. Occasional maneuvering may be required, but trained paddlers easily avoid rocks and medium-size waves. Swimmers are seldom injured, and while group assistance may be helpful, it's seldom needed.

Class III: Intermediate. Rapids have moderate, irregular waves that may be difficult to avoid and are large enough to swamp an open canoe or to wash over a sit-on-top. Complex maneuvers in fast current and good boat control in tight passages or around ledges are often required; large waves or strainers (any obstacle that allows water to pass through, such as a downed tree or a rock with a hole in it) may be present but are easily avoided. Strong eddies and powerful current effects may be found, especially on large-volume rivers. Scouting is advisable and is highly recommended for inexperienced parties or those without local knowledge. Self-rescue is easy, but group assistance is helpful to avoid long swims.

Class IV: Advanced. Intense, powerful, but predictable rapids requiring precise boat control in turbulent water. Waves may be large and unavoidable; holes or constricted passages demand quick maneuvering under pressure. Precise eddy turns are mandatory; a strong Eskimo roll is advisable. Scouting is needed for initial descents. Skilled and practiced group assistance for rescue may be required.

Class V: Expert. Extremely long, obstructed, or very violent rapids that expose a paddler to danger. Large, unavoidable waves, holes, or steep and congested chutes with complex routes. Rescue is difficult, even for trained experts.

Class VI: Extreme. The very limits of boatable water, with extreme difficulty, unpredictable routes, and a very high level of danger. Rescue may be impossible, and the consequences of error are extreme.

Putting your stern upstream and backpaddling works just as well, with a couple of exceptions. Paddling backward is not as efficient a stroke as forward, and you'll find it harder to see exactly where you're going. If you come around a bend and find half the river blocked, a back ferry is a neat way to orient yourself above a clear passage.

The river downstream is calling, so let's go. As you ferry out, reach out and plant a high brace on the downcurrent side of your sit-on-top ahead of the seat. The current will grab the blade and swivel you so that you turn downstream. You can also do a low brace on the downstream side behind the cockpit to achieve the same turn.

Your sit-on-top feels alive; it's quivering as all the changes in the current play on its hull. The more you paddle on rivers, the more you'll understand this language of motion. The river is telling you of changes in depths, of unseen bumps and hollows, of realignments of the main current, of changes in the speed of the current—and all are clues to what lies ahead.

Rivers are never straight, and you're coming up to the first bend. If you just drifted, you'd find yourself near the bank on the outside of the bend. The current will be faster on the outside, and the channel will be deeper. The river may even have undercut the bank on the outside. A tree or root wad being washed downstream will follow the main current and can hang up on the outside bank. If you know it's clear and safe, ride the faster water. If you have a question, you can easily back-ferry across the current to the inside of the bend where the water moves slower. The water will also be thinner, however, so watch that you don't bump.

Speaking of bumps, look over there where the surface of the river is humped up into one. Paddlers call this a pillow, and just upstream of it is an obstruction on the river bottom. It's probably a rock, and the current is deflected from the rock to create the smooth pillow. If the current is faster or the rock closer to the surface, there may be a turbulent area at the downstream side of the pillow, creating a "hole" in the water. Depending on the speed of the current and volume of water, this might be a recirculating eddy—which may be a nice place to park for a moment as you scout your route; but it also may be a deep, frothing hole that is a playground for expert paddlers only. It depends on the current.

If the rock sticks up above the surface, it will create an eddy or a hole on its downstream side. The current will bulge up into a pillow on the upstream face of the rock.

Take a good look at the pillow. It parts the current and creates a V pointing upstream. An upstream-pointing V marks an obstruction in the river. A V pointing downstream marks a passage between obstructions. Because of a change in current speed, a series of hydraulic waves—a wave train—often forms at the downstream apex of a V.

Rocks in the river are a paddler's best friends. While it is possible (and, as you'll learn, likely) to hit one, the rock divides the current, and you'll most likely be carried around the rock with the flow of the water. Eddies behind rocks are the stepping-stones that you use to hop down the river. However, you have to know the key to getting into an eddy.

You'll see a distinct line between the downstream current and the recirculating current flowing back into the eddy. That's the eddyline, and it will vary from a blurry area of tiny swirls to a sharp demarcation that can be inches high. Remember that bit about always leaning downcurrent? Crossing an eddyline means you're changing current flows and thus the direction of downcurrent. If you lean the wrong way, you can upset.

As you approach the eddy from upstream, swing your sit-on-top so that you're between 70 degrees and a right angle to the eddyline. Keep a good forward speed so that you cross the eddyline with enthusiasm. You should be aiming at the downstream face of the rock to enter the eddy as high as possible. The closer you are to the rock, the easier it is to turn. In fact, if you don't bump the rock a few times, you're not entering high enough or aggressively enough.

As your bow crosses the eddyline, reach forward in a high brace and plant your paddle as high in the eddy as you can. The eddy current will pull your paddle—and bow—toward the rock, and the main river current will push your stern downriver in the few seconds you'll spend crossing the eddyline. You'll pivot and come to rest in the shelter of the rock.

Leaving the eddy is almost the same. Accelerate up the eddy and cross the eddyline at anywhere from a 45-degree to a 90-degree angle, paddling aggressively. Plant a high brace off your bow on the downcurrent side as you cross the line, and the two currents will spin your sit-on-top around and send you off down the river.

Again, you're switching currents as you cross the line, so remember to lean downcurrent. You'll almost instinctively lean with your brace. (Sometimes you'll hear this bracing turn called a duffek; whitewater racer Milo Duffek revolutionized kayaking with this aggressive and precise turn.) What if you want to work your way back to the upcurrent end of a series of rocks? Well, you can land and carry your sit-on-top up the shore. You can also work your way from eddy to eddy by exiting one eddy and—instead of turning downstream—aggressively paddling upstream into the tail of the next eddy. This is called an attainment move.

The river current will flow around a rock, carrying you with it, but it will flow through the limbs and trunks of a tree toppled into the water. In the worst case the current will carry you into the tree, which will act just like a sieve and pinion you in the debris. The force of the river will try to hold you there. A tree or root wad is one of the most dangerous things you'll encounter on moving water. Simply put, avoid them.

By miscalculating, you can be swept sideways and "broach" on a rock. Every one of your instincts will tell you to lean away from the rock. If you do, however, the current will roll your boat over (more quickly than you can believe), and you and your sit-on-top will be upside down against the rock. Instead, aggressively lean toward the rock. That will present the smooth bottom of your sit-on-top to the current and lift the ends of it from the water. In most cases you'll be able to shove off and slide around the rock—or the current may even carry you around. If the boat is truly wedged, bail out. Don't risk entanglement.

If you are separated from your sit-on-top in the river, turn so that your head is upstream, and swim on your back (at an angle to the current) toward the most attainable bank. Keep your feet as close as possible to the surface of the water. You might slightly arch your back to keep your rump from hanging down and bumping. Just as with your sit-on-top, you're ferrying.

If you don't think about it, it's all too easy to allow your feet to dangle down. You're losing part of your swimming power but, more important, you also risk wedging a foot into a crack or under an obstruction on the bottom.

But none of these upsetting things happened to you today. You made a few turns into eddies, you ferried back and forth across the current, you bounced through waves at the bottom of a V, and you even back-ferried to find a better route down a V between two rocks. Now you're approaching your landing place, appropriately enough called the take-out. It should be out of the main thrust of the current, with a gently sloping beach (in a perfect world).

Swing around so that the bow of your sit-on-top points upstream, and ferry your way to the upcurrent end of the landing beach. That way, if you miscalculate the strength of the current, you won't be shoved past the take-out. Paddle until your bow bumps the shore, swing your foot over the side, and as you stand up remember to grab the toggle handle at the bow. You don't want your sit-on-top voyaging without you! Pull it up on the beach, leaving plenty of room for the following sit-on-tops to land; as soon as you have a friend available, the two of you should carry your boats up and out of the way.

Don't mistake these few words for a class in river running! Seek out and enjoy the best instruction from a qualified instructor, and paddle with a club of skilled paddlers. You'll learn more, and faster, in the wake of a good teacher than you possibly can on your own, and a band of paddlers will bolster your confidence on the river—and pluck you from the water when you exceed the envelope of your skill and ability.

Paddling the Seven Seas

Those who paddle sit-on-tops upon both the broad expanses of open water and the frothy joyrides of whitewater rivers are quick to differentiate between the two: Whitewater is reflexive paddling, responding almost instinctively to the challenges of the moment, while touring is a reflective, contemplative experience in which you assess the benefits of different courses of action and choose the one that works best for the particular combination of circumstances before you.

Okay, that's very simplified. That's the two ends of the sit-on-top paddling scale, and reality says that all paddling is somewhere on the balance beam between the two. Not only that, but we don't even have a good descriptive word for the paddling we mean when we talk about "ocean kayaking" or "kayak touring" or even "flatwater cruising." "Ocean kayaking" encompasses salt water and fresh; you can "tour" on river, lake, or ocean; and as anyone who has ventured out upon them in a small boat knows, there's nothing flat about oceans or big lakes.

For today, at least, I'll call "touring" that paddling on waters where wind is the dominant characteristic and you can paddle out of sight of the shore. What about waves, you ask? Imagine a swatch of velvet covered with cat hair. If you run your hand over the material, the cat hair will form long cylinders that roll over the velvet. Your hand is the wind, the cat hair is the pattern of energy the wind creates, and the velvet is the water. A wave is the up-and-down movement of water within the rolling cylinder.

Sit-on-top touring is a combination of paddling technique, route finding, and moving through surf. There's nothing magical or complicated about it, as long as you approach the water with respect and common sense. You've already worked your way through the basic paddling strokes, and while there are always further refinements and combinations to learn, they come with the pleasures of paddling. Route finding? At its simplest, it's just the art and craft of paddling your sit-on-top from where you are to the place you can see and want to be.

Surf, however, is the unknown and frightening bugaboo of many sit-on-top paddlers. Faced with the possibility of a breaking wave at their launch or take-out site, many paddlers simply shake their heads and abandon their paddling plans for the day. All because they haven't taken the time to understand the surf zone. And that's a pity, because the surf sculpts some of the most enchanting and rich shorelines imaginable. Now, I'm not talking about mondo surf pummeling the north coast of Oahu with 30-foot breakers. Surf can be a breaking wave from 2½ feet high—that's about eye level when you're sitting on the beach at the waterline—to 4 feet high, or eye level when you're on your knees.

Surf zone? Imagine a couple of cylinders of cat hair rolling in toward your beach. Water molecules at the top of each cylinder—okay, wave—are moving forward, toward the beach. Water molecules in the trough are moving back, away from the beach.

In deep water the cylinder just rolls along unimpeded. When the coil

Launching and landing are the two most potentially challenging, and the two most important, skills in ocean or touring paddling. Find a sheltered cove where the waves slide rather than break upon the beach.

Paddling on the ocean will bring you to some of the most incredibly dramatic and beautiful places on the planet, but remember to cautiously match your skills to the voyage.

of energy rolls up on a beach, though, it trips on the bottom and is unable to pick up enough water to keep the cylinder full. The front of the wave (the direction in which the energy is moving) starts to become convex, and the energy coil collapses.

If the underwater profile of the beach is long and shelving, the energy in the wave will dissipate over a long approach. The wave will go from a smooth hump in the water to a gentle peak, and a slow spillover of froth will slide down the front face.

If the underwater profile is abrupt, with a steeply inclined seafloor angling up from a deep approach, the energy coil—or wave—will trip suddenly. The wave will rapidly rise up, and the face will become an overhanging cliff that collapses in a crash and roar of spume.

Assuming the waves are the same size (that's a function of how strong the wind has been blowing, for how long, and over what reach or expanse of water), the same total amount of energy will be released at those two beaches. Over the gently sloped beach with the long approach, the energy release will be slow and controlled, and the paddling will be manageable. Over the steep beach the release will come explosively, all at once, and you'll be in adrenaline city.

Note that I'm not talking about the height of the wave here. A 2½-foot-high breaking wave can capsize you in an instant, while a 5-foot slumping wave can offer you a safe and fun ride right up to the edge of the dry sand. Begin your surf experience in small, slumping waves because these offer you the most time in which to react and the fewest surprises if you fail to react properly.

Learn to paddle in the "energy" zone, and all the coastlines are yours.

Launching

Rarely will you encounter waves coming straight onto the beach, and even more rarely will you encounter a perfectly straight beach. You'll see that the surf is less on the sides of a small cove or bay than directly in front of the mouth. A small point or jetty will provide shelter on its lee side. Bring your sit-on-top to the water's edge at one of these sort-of sheltered spots, and let's have some fun.

Start by sitting on the beach and looking—really looking—at the waves. Look immediately off your personal beach to spot any weird currents or spouts that may indicate a hidden obstruction, but concentrate your attention farther offshore to where the waves are really breaking. Some places may look like soup at a boil, full of froth and energy, while others seem to have a smaller break where it would be easier to punch through. Some of the waves will look bigger and will be breaking a bit farther offshore. If you can concentrate on watching for fifteen minutes or so, you'll start to see the shape of a pattern in the waves. It might be three bigger waves and four smaller ones, it might be that every ninth wave seems to tower over the others, it might . . . well, just look and observe. Sometimes the groups will be even and easy to see; sometimes they'll overlap. Under some circumstances you might even see two wave patterns crossing, and in doing so throwing up big humps. At other times—especially near cliffs—you will see wave energy reflected back from the shore, creating bigger and more confused breaks offshore.

Whatever the case, you will recognize that there are times in which the energy zone seems to quiet down. Such a time—when the surf zone is smaller and closer to the shore—is the target for which you are searching, and when it repeats you should be ready to shoot out.

Nervous? Why not? You're trying something new that will test your sit-on-top skills, you're paddling in a strange and powerful environment that doesn't seem to care if you're a paddler or a swimmer, and most of us have spent our whole lives demanding first-time perfection of ourselves. On the other hand, you're all set to experience something new that will expand your paddling skills; because you've thought to wear all the proper safety and thermal protection gear you need, it really doesn't matter if you take a quick swim (in fact, it might even feel good); and this first splashing launch into surf is a flailing step toward paddling perfection. In other words, cut yourself some slack, and remember that you're here for the fun of it.

You're also here with your sit-on-top, and sit-on-tops are much easier and faster to launch and board than their conventional hard-shelled kayak cousins. They are also a lot more comfortable (mentally as well as physically) and a fair bit safer when you do come a cropper. One of the truths about finding your paddling limits is that, yes, you can lean too far and exceed the stability of your brace. With a sit-on-top such a positive learning experience is followed by a few seconds of reboarding and more happy paddling.

As the set of waves you've been watching starts to subside, pull the bow of your sit-on-top just barely into the water so that the bow is floating but the stern remains on the beach. Tow it by the bow handle whenever in the surf. The boat will pivot like a weather vane in any moving water. If you're at the front and the stern is on the beach, any incoming water will keep the sit-on-top more or less in line. You really don't want to be pushing your sit-on-top from the middle, around the cockpit, and have the slap from an incoming wave turn your sit-on-top sideways between you and the wave; the wave will tumble the boat right over you. A good safety rule for any kind of water is this: *Always* be at the upstream/upcurrent end of your sit-on-top.

When the surf zone quiets down and you're mentally ready, pull your sit-on-top into about knee-deep water with the stern clear of the beach. In the same motion step over your sit-on-top with one leg, facing forward, and smoothly sit down in the cockpit. Smooth is the goal, but don't waste time or energy making it look graceful. With your sit-on-top still gliding forward directly at the waves, get your feet on board and drive forward with your most powerful paddle strokes.

The power position on your paddle is easy to find. Hold your paddle in both hands and lift it horizontally until it just clears the top of your head. Slide your hands out along the shaft until your upper arms are horizontal and straight out from your shoulders, and your forearms are vertical and form a 90-degree angle with your upper arms. Some paddlers will put a small piece of tape on the paddle shaft to mark where their little fingers should go, but that's an aid you'll soon outgrow as your muscles learn this power position.

"He who hesitates is lost" is never more true than when you are launching into the surf zone! Put your head down and drive straight into the incoming waves. That's straight into the waves and not straight out from the beach—because, as you've already seen, the waves rarely march directly in parallel to the shoreline. If you keep driving, you can power through most of the waves that haven't broken. Depending on their size

The quickest way to board when you're heading into the surf is to step over your sit-on-top, scoot it forward, and sit down as the seat passes you.

and your aggressiveness, you can also drive through the vast majority of waves that have already collapsed and are sluicing toward shore in a welter of foam or have merely slumped into foam. A bigger wave or an onrush of foaming water may slow you or may even wash you a bit backward, but if you keep driving toward the open water, the wave will pass under you.

Okay, so you're doing well—but all of a sudden you realize this set of waves isn't cooperating. A massive wave (2 feet can look massive when you're paddling) has popped up right in front of you, and its concave face is about to seriously dump on you. On the plus side, you're filled with adrenaline and everything looks much bigger than it really is; from a sitting perspective even a small wave appears mountainous. Besides that, you can't wish yourself somewhere else. Stick your chin down on your chest, lean forward, and increase your paddling power. You have your head down in this forward lean for a very good reason—you don't want to be slapped in the chest and face as your bow knifes into the wave. The impact of the water on that broad surface will at best slow you—and may very well drive you backward—and it will disturb your paddling rhythm at a time you really need to keep paddling. If you manage to keep your balance and your direction, you'll almost always paddle right on through the wave.

Worst case? You're sitting in the trough, being sucked right into a breaking wave that's falling in your lap. If you lift your paddle from the water, shut your eyes, and freeze, you may fall out of your sit-on-top. (Do the same thing in absolutely flat water and you might also topple out, for that matter.) Either reboard and try again (it will be harder, from having no forward speed and being tossed about in the waves), or swim back to shore, pushing your sit-on-top while rehearsing the story you'll tell on yourself.

The fact is, you should deliberately go swimming in the surf a few times. You'll become intimately acquainted with its power and quirks, a great deal of its mystery will be dispelled, and you'll most likely become a better paddler.

I didn't mention this as you launched, but don't paddle alone. As a rule, three boats are a good minimum. When you're learning surf skills, you'll be more comfortable and a lot safer if your two companions are very experienced as paddlers, as instructors, and in surf rescue. Down the road you'll pass along the same favor to other newcomers to the sport.

Returning to Shore

Wow, in the face of all that confronted you, you survived. You made it. You're out on the deep, with the rolling waves slowly lifting and dropping you as you paddle along. You rise to the top of an incredible coil of energy and slide down its face with as close to a feeling of flying as you can find while still on the surface of this globe. Today you can paddle for miles with little effort—the wind and gravity propel you effortlessly along. The only problem is that sometime before it gets dark, you'll want to return to the land.

Remember the first thing you did when you came to the beach? That's right! You sat out there on the waves and took a long, careful look at the surf zone.

Here's something to think about before you launch: The sheer face of an oncoming wave looks much higher than the smooth slope of the back side of a wave. In other words, the view out is more exciting than the view in. The perspective is different.

As you bob up and down on your sit-on-top, study the surf zone for a while. You'll see the high-energy zone forming with all its froth and tumult. Identify where the whitewater begins. Now—working slowly and keeping your sit-on-top under control—paddle up to the edge of the surf zone. Charge in and the surf will catch you; you'll be surfing under marginal control in a wild ride toward the beach—even on a 2-foot wave. If you edge in cautiously, you can back out with your stern knifing through the first rise of each wave.

Want to avoid going for an unexpected ride? Angle across the waves at 30 to 45 degrees. That will give you a good view of the beach, the

Launching and Landing Tips

◆ Don't launch from or land on a beach filled with swimmers. Even a light, very controllable sit-on-top packs a terrible wallop to someone in the water.

◆ If you can possibly avoid it, don't launch or land on a beach marked with rocks, boulders, or logs at the waterline. These are hazards you don't need to face. A floating log is a disaster just waiting to happen!

◆ Without plenty of practice, don't launch or land in slumping surf larger than 2 to 3 feet. Sure, it can be done and done safely, but you need plenty of practice before you star in a concert!

◆ You might launch from a shallow beach at low tide with an easy, slumping surf—but return at higher tide with a breaking surf crashing on a steep beach. Conditions change, so beware.

◆ An offshore wind tends to keep the surf down; an onshore wind tends to build the surf up. When you launch, consider the likely weather conditions at your landing site.

◆ Waves look much bigger from the front than the back. Conditions might appear pretty good as you approach a beach, only to turn frightening once you're in the surf zone.

◆ There's never, ever any reason to paddle out into surf you fear is beyond your capabilities. If you have any questions, sit on the beach and enjoy the view.

waves, and your position, yet still allow you to retreat if the situation looks beyond your control.

Just as you did before you launched, identify the pattern of the waves rolling in toward the beach. Once you've spotted the progression, pick out the next-to-smallest wave in a decreasing chain. This should be one that breaks closest to the beach.

Follow just behind this wave as it starts toward the beach. Snuggle in behind it with your bow up on its shoulders. You'll think, visually, that you're paddling uphill, while in fact you're riding the coil of energy rolling toward the shore. Your stern will be dragging in the trough, and the energy in the trough will be flowing out toward the following wave. If you're balanced between the two, it will be relatively easy to keep your sit-on-top heading shoreward.

If you drop back off your wave into the following trough, you're likely to be sucked into the face of the following wave.

This is bad berries. You have water cascading down the face of one wave, pushing on the stern of your sit-on-top with significant force. At the same time the bow of your boat is in the counterenergy flow of the trough, pushing back on the front of your boat. The most common result is a dramatic and sudden twisting of your sit-on-top sideways, dropping you parallel to the face of the incoming wave. Technically, it's a broach. Practically, it's a terrifying switch of position with no control, and it normally leads immediately to a capsize. If you're in Hawaii you can call it a *huli*, which means the same thing for your sit-on-top and also deposits you in the water.

If you think rather than react, you'll be okay. Every instinct you have is to lean away from the face of that wave. The only trouble is that if you do so, you're tilting your deck and gunwales toward the onrushing current and the water will grab you and turn you over. The energy force in the trough is directed toward the face of the following wave. The proper course of action is to jam your paddle directly into the face of the wave and lean on it in a low brace. On a low wave some paddlers will reach over the crest with a high brace and lock onto the rear face of the wave. The low brace will work on just about every occasion.

Lean into the wave! The soup rolling down the face of the wave will shove you along sideways toward the shore. All things considered, you're likely to stay upright on your sit-on-top on this wild ride unless you go out of your way to fight the boat.

Keep your paddle low. The low brace, with your hands over the top of the paddle shaft, will give you immense stability and won't force your hands and paddle shaft higher than your shoulders. Mechanically, you're not designed to cope with the potential stresses of a braced paddle with your hands higher than your shoulders. You face the very real risk of a dislocated shoulder.

One of the major advantages of a sit-on-top is that you're likely to be lifted right off your boat before you can put excessive stress on your paddle—and thus your shoulder. If you have an impressive brace and the skill to control it, consider knee straps. They will lock you into your boat but free you the moment you relax your legs and feet in the footwells. Squeeze your knees together (against the straps) for more control, or relax and straighten your knees to bail out.

You're going to be better off approaching the beach at an angle. If you come straight in, your bow will ground and your stern will pivot around. With luck your sit-on-top will remain sunny-side up, but luck is a fragile reed. If you land at a 30- to 45-degree angle to the beach—you're riding the wave right in, but your sit-on-top is at an angle to the wave—you're more likely to make a smooth landing without a precipitous broach.

I'd rather land with my bow pointing upbeach than with it pointing away from the shore. I think I get a softer, more controlled landing. On the other hand, sometimes you just do whatever is possible.

Once you've landed—straight in, at an angle, or sideways—you have one more thing to remember: Get out on the surf side of your sit-on-top. You learned earlier never to be on the downstream/downcurrent side of your sit-on-top, and landing is one of the easiest places to forget this lesson. Your legs are going to be tired, and you may well be chilled. If you leap out on the beach side of your sit-on-top, the next wave will lift your hull and slam it into your shins. If it's a little wave, a few inches high, your friends will be surprised at your vocabulary. If it's a bigger wave (even slightly bigger), it will knock you down and roll your sit-on-top right up your legs. That's a heck of a way to mar an otherwise great landing.

Safety Rules

Common sense, they say, is an uncommon virtue—and yet common sense is the most basic and valuable of all the tools you can carry when you venture out upon the waters. Yes, there are hazards upon the sea, the rivers, and the lakes. The waters are not so much unforgiving as they are distantly uncaring. And the lure of paddling upon them is in no small way the assumption of the responsibility for your own self. You set your own course, you determine your passages, and you are ultimately responsible for the success of your voyage.

Keep your common sense at the front of your mind. Learn the skills for the boating you will love, and in doing so honestly assess the level of your skills. Do not be led by others into waters beyond your skills—and know that on one day you may be an awesome master of the water and on the next, a feather being blown across the surface. Know the laws, the regulations, and the safety standards for the waters you choose to travel.

Learn, under the guidance of a qualified instructor, paddling techniques, water safety, and first aid. And know that learning is a journey and not a destination. There are always more lessons.

Know the capacities of your sit-on-top. Carefully inspect your personal flotation device, your sit-on-top, your paddle, and your safety equipment before each launch.

Wear your personal flotation device. Sure, the U.S. Coast Guard requires you to carry one aboard your kayak whenever you're afloat, and numerous local authorities require you to wear it. The truth is that your PFD will help keep your head above water—but only if you are wearing it. In the unlikely but always possible event of a mishap, your PFD may also add insulation to your body and protect you from the chill of the water.

Sit-on-top kayaking simply does not mix with either alcohol or drugs (prescription or not).

Paddling on rivers or in the surf zone is potentially dangerous. Always wear a properly fitting watersports helmet in whitewater.

Don't concentrate so completely on your paddling and sit-on-top that you are oblivious to weather conditions and water temperatures. Onshore and offshore winds switch with the time of day; a beach that may have been sheltered from the surf in the morning may be exposed to crashing waves with a change in the wind or the cycle of the tides in the afternoon. Fog, rain, or squalls can blow in with surprising speed. At all times while paddling, keep in mind an immediate route or landing to get off the water as weather or water conditions change.

Prepare yourself for changes in weather as well as the possibility of capsizing. When paddling in cold weather or in cold waters, ensure your comfort with a wet suit or a dry suit. In balmy temperatures and in the full light of the sun, shelter yourself with a long-sleeved shirt, a broad-brimmed or skirted hat, and leg coverings.

Know the waters upon which you venture. Glean all the information you can from charts and guidebooks, and when paddling in a new area, turn to local sit-on-top paddlers for site-specific information on currents, weather patterns, shoreline conditions, and less obvious hazards

Last, but by no means least, file a "float plan" with your family or friends. Describe where you are going, your activities, how many people and boats will be in the party, the colors and shapes of your sit-on-tops, and how long you expect to be gone. Give yourself a generous but realistic cushion for the delays that can overtake any group of sit-on-toppers. Then stick to your plan. Always contact the person holding your float plan when you return home.

Following these simple steps won't make you a fuddy-duddy on the water, but it will expand your boating opportunities and help make your sit-on-top voyages safer and more fun.

What do you say? In these pages, you've had an introduction to the wide world of sit-on-top kayaking. You don't need more words, just a long spate of paddle strokes to reawaken the water skills you already knew you had but seem to have forgotten. It's a great day; let's go for a paddle.

Index

About the Author

Dennis Stuhaug has been paddling the rivers, lakes, and salt water of North America as a trip leader, instructor, and guide for more than fifty years. He has served as the editor of *Canoe & Kayak* magazine and as a consultant on boating safety to state and national agencies. In addition to *Sit-on-Top Kayaking,* Dennis has published *Kayaking Made Easy* with The Globe Pequot Press and has written numerous articles on paddling and paddle sports. He lives, writes, and paddles on Puget Sound in Washington State.